Traditional Bakery Cookbook

ISBN: 978-1-964712-27-7

DEDICATIONS

<u>My boys</u>

Dustin & Quinton,

My inspiration, my drive, my purpose. You give me focus and motivate me to push through apprehension, self-doubt and exhaustion. You're my first thought when I wake up in the morning and my last before I fall asleep each night. For years, literally the only two reasons I got out of bed in the morning. Now, that you're both grown and out on your own, it's turned into the sound of dogs barking to go out in the morning...either way. I'm up.

The girl

Penny Thorne grew up in Westerly, RI along the CT border: She was a rebellious tomboy and spent most of her time wandering around and exploring the environment as a loner: She had a deep love and respect for animals and the environment, people not so much: Penny began working with animal rescues at the age of 12 and continues to this day: While growing up her two best friends and biggest influencers in her life were her maternal grandparents: She lived with them off and on during her childhood and young adult years: Penny's grandparent's home was always filled with music, laughter and calorie counting since both she and her grandmother, aka "Grimace" were both a little on the chubby side and enjoyed following all the newest diet fads: Her Gramps, affectionately referred to as "Cramps" taught her a valuable life lessons; to be confident, resilient and that anything is possible by instilling a "never give up on yourself and you're never too old to do anything" attitude:

Some would say I've done ok, for a girl...

FORWARD

"Enjoy Your Mistakes, That's What Separates You From The Rest Of The World"

Marilyn Manson

My entire life has been full of mistakes. I revel in my mistakes and hope the trend will continue. I find my mistakes comforting and uplifting. They are where I have learned the most about myself and they have provided me with a strong foundation and sense of self. Afterall, there's nothing better than a heaping slice of humble pie to start the day off right.

Table OF Contents

ABOUT THE AUTHOR

Penny Thorne was raised in Westerly and developed a passion for art at a young age. When she was 16, she got a part-time job working as a cupcake decorator where she discovered that art isn't just for the eyes — it's also for the taste buds! Penny earned a degree in Baking & Pastry, along with Food Service Management at Johnson Wales University in 2000. Over the course of her career, Penny has managed multiple bakeries and developed a fondness for teaching her craft to pastry students and home bakers alike. In the summer of 2019, Penny opened Black Dahlia Baking Company with a focus on accommodating the custom requests of her community, whether dietary or decorative. Her bakery proudly offers daily vegan, sugar-free, and gluten-free options. Penny also specializes in wedding cakes, custom creations for all occasions along with teaching private baking classes and hosting children's decorating parties. When Penny is not baking, she enjoys spending time with her two grown sons, Dustin and Quinton, their wives and her awesome grandchildren.

Black Dahlia Baking Company is a custom bake shop originating only a few blocks away from the historic downtown area where Pawcatuck CT & Westerly RI meet. The owner is Pastry Chef Penny Thorne who grew up in Westerly RI and has been working in food service for over 40 years where she started out working 50 hours a week as a fast food service manager making $6.00 an hour at an ice cream shop located at Misquamicut Beach when she was just a teenager, 13 years of age.

This first job not only taught her responsibility and good work ethic and illegal practices it also sparked an interest, desire and passion that would grow and develop over the years into an entire career based around the food service industry. Over the years Penny has worked in all aspects of the baking industry both back of the house and front. She has also helped design and manage several well-known bakeries throughout both CT & RI.

Penny is also a natural artist and has a strong appreciation for symmetry, color and design and strives to bring her creative flair to each of her delicious creations:

(Black Dahlia Baking Company has been operating as a side hustle for several years until it finally developed into a full-time gig about 6 years ago when Penny moved back to the area after living and working in Providence, RI for 20 years):

Bakeries may differ in many ways but the one commonality they all have in common is that they don't easily substitute or individualize customer requests be it dietary or design: It is for this reason that Pastry Chef Penny Thorne of Black Dahlia Baking Company has made it her core mission to offer absolutely **NO DIETARY RESTRICTIONS:** Essentially giving the customer full empowerment to pick and choose the ingredients that will be used to create their very own customizable edible creation: Not only does she offer and cater to all dietary requests; she does this while also individualizing desserts based on your specific theme:

To view the menu and online gallery please like and follow the bakery Facebook page:

The Business of Baking:
Black Dahlia Baking Co. owner ready for any challenge.

Penny Thorne works on decorating freshly baked cookies in the kitchen on Wednesday, November 6, 2019. Thorne has opened a new bakery on South Broad Street in Pawcatuck that caters not only to typical sweet lovers, but also to the keto, vegan, and gluten-free crowd. Harold Hanka, The Westerly Sun

STONINGTON — Penny LaPietra Thorne bent over a tray of freshly-baked shortbread cookies in her tidy, eclectic bakery-kitchen on a recent afternoon last week thoughtfully decorating each one with an intricate, curly-cue design.

"Sometimes I have a plan and sometimes I don't," said Thorne as she squeezed the pastry bag full of frosting in swirling patterns. "This is just fun for me."

Thorne, a Westerly native, owns the Black Dahlia Baking Company on South Broad Street. She opened her small business last summer and, as the executive bakery chef, has been creating traditional and unusual baked goods for customers ever since.

"I'm a one woman show," said a smiling Thorne, who is friendly, talkative and warm. "And I'm an artist too. I paint every day."

Thorne, who also makes custom wedding cakes and plans to offer baking classes beginning in the new year, said she delights in a good challenge. If a customer has a dietary restriction or food allergy, she'll find a way to meet their needs.

> ***"This is my little laboratory," she said with a laugh, "I can create anything a customer requests."***

"I have one customer who orders gluten-free sourdough bread each week," she said. "And I make things for people on Weight Watchers too."

Thorne, who graduated from Westerly High School in 1985, and earned a bachelor's degree in bakery and pastry from Johnson & Wales University in 2000, has been in the food service since she was a 13-year-old.

"I worked in Misquamicut at a little place which has since become the Purple Ape," she recalled. Then it was on to Scott's Supermarket when she was 15, where she became a cupcake decorator.

"I've always baked, and I've always created art," said Thorne, the mother of two sons, Dustin and Quinton. "I paint every day."

After teaching at Johnson & Wales, and a 30-plus-year career that included overseeing bakeries such as Olga's Cup & Saucer in Providence, and Sweet Cakes in Peace Dale as well as a seven-day-a-week schedule, Thorne decided it was time to move back to the area and open her own bakery. Thorne

said she looked at a number of locations, but when she met her former landlady, Elizabeth Mitchell-Cipriano, she knew she found the perfect spot. Mitchell-Cipriano owns the building at 210 South Broad Street that houses her business, Handlebar Café, as well as Thorne's Black Dahlia Baking Company and Coco's Salon, which is owned by Mitchell-Cipriano's sister, Stephanie Shawn.

"From the minute I met her I knew," said Thorne. "We're like a family. Three women with small businesses. We're all very supportive of one another."

"We hit it off immediately," Mitchell-Cipriano said. "We've become business sisters."

Mitchell-Cipriano said she's thrilled to give another woman the chance to run her own business and be her own boss. "She's got such pride and dedication," Mitchell-Cipriano. "She's great for business but not so much my waistline. I've already ordered three pies for Thanksgiving ... and cookies too." "I like to say I'm the sugar to their spice," Thorne said with a laugh.

> ***When it came to naming her new place, Thorne thought of her grandfather, Anthony Lionetti, the man who taught her to garden.***

The man who called the dahlia his favorite flower. He was "the most supportive and influential person in my life growing up," said Thorne. "We earned our Master Gardener certificates from URI together in 1985 and I continue to garden and grow dahlias because it's my way of having him with me each day," she said. Kerry Vacca of

Westerly, one of Thorne's regular customers, said after seeing photos of Black Dahlia goodies on Facebook, she knew she had to make a visit.

> *"I walked out of her bakery with about 10 different cookies and various types of baked goods," said Vacca, a nurse, in an email message. "A few of them never made it home."*

Vacca said she was so impressed that she asked Thorne to make special "nurse" cookies to share with her colleagues at the hospital.

"I swear, the detail in the cookies was amazing," she said. "I cannot even tell you how much those cookies were loved by my co-workers. They were devoured." After that, she said, she ordered raspberry-filled "Funny Bones," another Black Dahlia specialty.

"I make a lot of retro cereal cakes" Thorne laughed, taking down a box of Peanut Butter Cap'n Crunch cereal. "I've made orders using Fruit Loops, Cookie Crunch and Cocoa Puffs Cereal. "

Ursula Ahern of Westerly has become a regular customer at the Black Dahlia Baking Company.

"I try to stay away, but her cream puffs are the best I have ever had," said Ahern with a chuckle.

"I also make pup cakes for dogs" said Thorne, who has been involved with Pit Bull rescue for decades and currently owns five dogs. "I have a lot of dog customers. Dogs have checkbooks too."

"Whatever people want me to do, I'll try to do," she said, "and I also make suggestions ... people tell me what ingredients they like, and I'll come up with ideas."

In the end, she said, it's all about customer service and going the extra mile.

On the inside of her left forearm, Thorne has tattooed a Sanskrit saying placed so she can look down and read it easily. "It means 'I am enough,'" Thorne said with a smile, adding, "I am. I am enough and sometimes I'm too much. Either way, I'm good with who I am."

Nancy B. Fusaro, Westerly Sun

WHY BLACK DAHLIA?

The name "Black Dahlia Baking Company" originated from a culmination of several ideas. The quick explanation is that both of my sons and I have always been into true crime, campy horror flicks, cults, graphic fantasies and music. We enjoy updating each other on the gruesome facts learned from reading and researching articles, watching the latest docuseries or by keeping up with newly discovered trivial revelations pertaining to the most notorious serial killers, cult leaders, mobsters, cartel and gang leaders. We have also attended several concerts together. My oldest son has also been a longtime fan of the **"BLACK DAHLIA MURDER"** death metal band from Michigan which also brings me back around to another infamous and unsolved true crime from 1947, **"THE BLACK DAHLIA MURDER"** of Elizabeth Short.

Stay Tuned For "The Murderous Version" Of This Cookbook - Already In The Works And Coming Soon To A Book Store Near You!

The longer and expanded upon version is that I grew up spending a lot of time with my maternal grandfather, I know, I know again with this guy... Anthony C. Lionetti, Jr. A lot of who I am today stems from the time, energy and devotion that my wonderful and irreplaceable grandfather so graciously gave to me.

> *My grandfather, "Cramps" as I liked to call him... had a tremendous influence on me while I was growing up and getting into trouble.*

He devoted countless hours teaching me how to be independent and self-sufficient by showing me how to do things like cooking, budgeting, tinkering with radio repair, solar panels, dandelion wine making, simple carpentry and plumbing and how to hook up a CB radio and speak secret trucker lingo to tractor trailer drivers traveling all over the US.

He even gave me private music lessons and taught me how to play the theme to "JAWS" & "Doe a Deer a Female Deer" on the piano while he stood behind me and played the trumpet.

Together we enjoyed looking at vintage military maps and organizing wooden pennies while listening to talk radio and big band sounds on the ol' Victrola. My gramps impressed upon me that you're never too old to stop learning and that I should always work on bettering myself and skills. We even took several night classes together at local high schools as part of the CCRI extension program and an extensive Master Gardener and Botany class at the University of Rhode Island. Above all, the times that I enjoyed the most were the days we spent together in his garden. We grew fruits, flowers, vegetables and often experimented with splicing different plants together to create our own hybrids.

One of my grandfather's favorite flowers to grow were dahlias, and yes, you guessed it, the third reason why I decided to go with the name 'BLACK DAHLIA BAKING COMPANY". I'd say that choosing the name was the easiest, most memorable way that I could come up with to honor the three most important and influential men in my life, my sons and my grandfather.

How to use this book

When I first wrote this book, I had grand ideas of it being more than just a simple cookbook; I wanted it to be a reference guide and learning tool that anyone could use, enjoy and benefit from; Whether it be a novice home baker, an excited teenager, homemaker or a professional chef working several years in the industry looking for outside inspiration; I wanted to somehow incorporate all my years of behind-the-scenes bakery knowledge and make things easier for my readers by debunking all the stupid and unnecessary steps that just waste time and cause frustration in the kitchen; I also thought it would be great to break each formula down and convert it into the three standard units of measure because not everyone utilizing these recipes are going to be using the same measurement system (Imperial, Metric or good 'ol pounds & ounces) And that's what I did, and it was a lot of work; But now, three years later, having spoken to all experience levels of bakers, I was forced to come to the realization that no one really cares; I also had a former boss who told me almost daily that my job was so easy a monkey could do it; So, there's also that However, I still held on to the idea for quite a while and wasted a lot of time by still writing each page that way because I thought it was innovative and intelligent; Until one morning I woke up and boom, it was decided; I needed to get rid of all that intelligentness; I deleted the unnecessary units and settled with just using the Imperial method of measuring in this book, i;e;; measuring cups and measuring spoons; And for all I know, monkeys could be the next generation of scratch bakers, who really knows? Don't worry, if you still want to know how to convert any recipe from one unit of measure to another, you'll soon be able to obtain a copy of the "MURDEROUS" uncensored and expanded version of this cookbook; That book contains three times the information as this book;

FACT: No Algebra Was Used When Making This Book; In Fact, Nothing Over 3rd Grade Math Was Used When Making This Book;

Finally, and most importantly, each recipe in this book can be converted from Traditional to Gluten Free, Dairy Free or Vegan by just substituting the ingredient you don't want to use from the base recipe by exchanging it with a substitution of your choice at the same ratio from the handy dandy substitution chart provided;

There are a few exceptions to this rule and those recipes have been effectively noted with the appropriate conversions;

Ingredient Substitution Guide

Chicken Eggs

Substitutions: Aquafaba 3 Tablespoons = 1 egg

Flax Seeds, 1 Tablespoons ground Flax plus 3 Tablespoons water = 1 egg

Liquid Egg Replacement, Vegan Powdered Egg Replacement – follow manufacturer's instructions

Yogurt – ¼ cup of Greek yogurt = 1 egg

All Purpose Flour

Even Exchange

Substitution: Gluten Free Flour (must say 1-1 for proper exchange)

Milk & Buttermilk

Even Exchange

Any Dairy Free Milk such as, Almond, Cashew, Coconut, Oat, Rice or Soy

Butter

(Follow manufacturer's instructions for proper exchange)

Applesauce, Coconut Oil, Margarine, Shortening, Vegan Butter

Honey

Even Exchange

Agave, Date or Maple Syrups

Cream Cheese

Even Exchange

Greek Yogurt, Sour Cream, Dairy Free or Vegan Cream Cheese

Additive Ideas & Exchanges:

Vanilla extract can be exchanged with any flavor extract providing it is exchanged at the same amount.

Fresh fruit should be exchanged with similar fruits such as apples & pears, oranges, grapefruits, lemons & limes, berries with berries, melons with melons, etc. If you mix up the even exchanges you may need to adjust and pull back some of the liquid content of your recipe. For example, exchanging oranges for pears in a muffin batter will add more liquid to the recipe due to the higher content of juice contained in the orange segments.

"Buttermilk" can be made with any milk by adding 1 tablespoon of acid such as white vinegar or lemon juice to one cup of milk. Let rest for 15-30 minutes to allow for the chemical process to breakdown and curdle the milk. Thus "softening" your recipe.

Zests can be substituted for liquid extracts at 1 Tablespoon of zest in exchange for 1 teaspoon of extract.

Typically, a bakery recipe can accommodate 1-2 cups of dry or liquid free additives without breaking the ingredient ratio and ruining the recipe.

Crushed cookies and dried cake crumbs can be exchanged for graham cracker crumbs when making crusts. Both Traditional and Gluten Free products work equally well.

BREAKFAST
PASTRIES

Is breakfast really the most important meal of the day? I think not, but for the sake of this section — let's agree to pretend.

Breakfast literally means "to break the fast" of not eating for several hours or overnight. No more, no less.

Apple Bread Pudding

Yield: (1) 9-inch square pan

(6-12) servings depending on how you score the pan:

This is a great way to use up day-old bread, croissants, raisin bread, danish or rolls of any size. You can also save all of the ends from any uneaten bread in a one-gallon zip lock bag and store it in the freezer until you have enough for this recipe. The same ends can also be used to make croutons and bread crumbs for homemade meatballs. Bread pudding is awesome, served at room temperature or warmed up and topped with whipped cream, caramel sauce or your favorite full fat ice cream.

Ingredients

Bread, baker's choice	10 cups, heaping	Eggs, large	6 each
Cream, heavy or whipping	2 cups	Extract, vanilla	1 tablespoon
Sugar, granulated	1 cup	Spice, cinnamon	1 teaspoon
Sugar, brown	½ cup	Apples, Granny Smith	2 cups, chopped
Salt	½ teaspoon	Additives: nuts, baking chips	1 cup

Method of Prep:

Preheat oven to 325'f

1. Slice the bread into cubes first. Then measure out your heaping cups and place into a large mixing bowl. Set aside until needed.

2. Prepare the apples by peeling, coring and dicing into rough chunks. Add the apples and any additives to the bread cubes and toss lightly to combine. Let sit while preparing the liquid below.

3. Measure out the remaining ingredients and gently whisk together until fully combined.

4. Pour the custard over the bread cube mixture and let sit for at least 30 minutes allowing the bread mixture to absorb the flavorful custard. Overnight is better if time permits.

5. Pour the mixture into an 9 inch square baking pan that has been sprayed with pan release and lightly press the bread cubes down so they are drowning under the custard.

6. Bake on 325'f for 65 minutes or until a toothpick comes out clean when inserted into the center diagonally.

7. Let cool completely before cutting, topping and serving.

Baker's Tip: The Bread Pudding Will Puff Up During Baking And Settle Itself Back Down Once Cooled.

Blackberry Poppy Oat Biscuits

Yield: (6-8) biscuits, using a 3-inch round cutter:

Wholesome & tender, flavor packed biscuits. They can be made into a variety of flavor combinations and served as is or warmed and topped with fruity preserves. And when you need more, and you will, this recipe is easy enough to double.

Ingredients

Flour, all purpose	3 cups	Oats, quick cooking	1 cup
Sugar, granulated	½ cup	Honey	¼ cup
Baking powder	3 teaspoons	Spice, cinnamon	1 teaspoon
Baking soda	1 teaspoon	Extract, vanilla	1 tablespoon
Salt	¾ teaspoon	Seeds, poppy	2 teaspoons
Butter, unsalted	1 ½ sticks	Blackberries	1 cup
Buttermilk	¾ cup	Zest, orange	1 tablespoon

Method of prep:

Preheat oven to 325'f

1. Scale out all ingredients.

2. Place all of the dry ingredients into a large bowl and add softened butter.

3. Mix by continuously pressing the butter through your fingers into the dry ingredients until a coarse & crumbly mixture remains.

4. Add in the oats, zest, berries and extract. Mix lightly by hand to incorporate.

5. Make a well in the center and pour in the buttermilk & honey.

6. Lift and press the mixture into itself until you can form one soft slightly dry dough mound.

7. Turn out onto a floured surface and press into a flat oval shape about 1 inch in thickness. You will need to dust your hands with flour lightly as needed to help reduce the stickiness of the honey.

8. Stamp out with a 2- or 3-inch round biscuit cutter and place onto a bare sheet tray that has been generously sprayed with pan release.

9. Prepare the top wash by combining 2 tablespoons of honey with 2 tablespoons of buttermilk and brush over the top of each biscuit.

10. Sprinkle a few oats on top and place the tray into the oven.

11. Bake on 325'f for 30-35 minutes. Serve warmly with butter, preserves, curds or honey.

Baker's Tip: You Can Soften Butter By Zapping In The Microwave For Short Bursts Like 10-20 Seconds At A Time Or Leaving It Out On The Counter The Night Before Using.

Blueberry Sour Cream
Coffee Cake Muffins

This recipe produces a wonderfully tasty muffin that can easily be baked into a coffee cake, quick bread or even a birthday cake just by changing out the pan used. All of which freeze well and can be easily thawed by pulling from the freezer and leaving wrapped on the kitchen counter to defrost overnight. Not a fan of sour cream? Just switch it out with softened cream cheese or plain Greek yogurt.

Ingredients

Muffins

Flour, all-purpose	2 ½ cups	Salt	¼ teaspoon
Sugar, brown	½ cup	Milk, whole	1 cup
Sugar, granulated	½ cup	Oil, vegetable	¾ cup
Baking powder	2 teaspoons	Eggs, large	2 each
Spice, cinnamon	1 teaspoon	Cream, sour	¼ cup
Baking soda	½ teaspoon	Fruit, berries	2 cups

Streusel Topping

Sugar, granulated	½ cup	Butter, unsalted	1 stick
Sugar, brown	½ cup	Flour, all purpose	1 ½ cups
Spice, cinnamon	1 teaspoon	Oats, quick	2 cups
Salt	½ teaspoon		

Quick Icing

Sugar, confectioner's	1 cup
Extract, vanilla	2 teaspoons
Cream, heavy or whipping	¼ cup

Baker's Tip: *Prepare Both The Streusel Topping And Quick Icing Ahead And Store In Airtight Containers Until Needed.*

Method of Prep:

Preheat oven to 325°f

Streusel

1. Combine the sugars, cinnamon & salt in a bowl and paddle on speed 1 to combine.

2. Add in the pre-softened butter and continue paddling.

3. Attach the bowl collar, (if using one, if not, good luck) and add the flour and oats. Paddle on low speed until combined.

4. Package in an airtight container and store in the refrigerator or freezer until needed.

Quick Icing

1. Place all ingredients into the mixing bowl and paddle until combined. This step can also be done by hand in a small bowl using a hand whisk.

2. Icing can be stored in the refrigerator or freezer until needed with an expiration date matching the date on the container of cream or other perishable liquid used to make.

Muffins

1. Combine all the dry ingredients into a mixing bowl fitted with the paddle attachment and paddle on speed 1 just to combine and help distribute the baking chemicals evenly.

2. Slowly add in the wet ingredients one at a time while continuing to paddle on speed Stop and scrape halfway through.

3. Turn the mixer off and remove the bowl. Fold in the fruit and/or additives by hand using a rubber spatula and fold lifting from the bottom center several times just enough to combine.

4. Scoop the batter into paper lined muffin pans with a level green handled scoop or fill with a standard kitchen spoon leaving about a ¼ inch gap between muffin batter and top of paper liner.

5. Top with the desired amount of streusel topping, sanding sugar and or additional fruit pieces and put into the oven to bake for approximately 25-30 minutes or until the toothpick tester comes out clean.

Baker's Tip: Depending on the way your oven distributes heat, you may need to rotate the pan halfway though baking to avoid ending up with uneven coloring or slanted muffin tops.

Allow the muffins to cool before drizzling with the icing or it will just absorb in and become invisible or possibly run off the muffin without sticking.

Variations:

1. Streusel can be added to the center of the muffins by splitting your scoop amount in half when filling the muffin cup and layering with streusel before scooping more muffin batter on top of it.

2. Substitute different fruits, nuts, chips, etc. to change the flavor.

3. If the muffin is too sweet for you, half of the sugar can be pulled out of the recipe, or you can substitute with a sugar alternative like stevia by following the conversion instructions on the product label.

Espresso Chocolate
Chip Bundt Cake

Yield: (1) standard 9 inch round bulked up bundt cake

Or (16) standard size muffins

Versatile and fun! Dust with powdered sugar, drizzle with melted chocolate ganache or peanut butter or, or, orrrrr make a sweetened glaze by whisking 2 cups of confectioner's sugar with 2 ounces of any hot liquid of your choice; milk, cream, muscle milk, iced coffee in the carton, flavored alcohols, juice or even preserves can act as a liquid when heated and whisked with confectioner's sugar. Other flavor options include adding 1 tablespoon zest, extract, spices, poppy, instant powders either to the batter itself or the glaze. Yet another fun flavor idea is to top with crushed candies, candy canes, cereal, mini chips (chocolate, white, butterscotch, etc…) the possibilities are endless! No matter which flavor combination your finished product is sure to be a delicious delight!

Ingredients

BUNDT

Butter, unsalted	2 sticks
Sugar, granulated	1 ½ cups
Eggs, large	4 each
Extract, vanilla	1 tablespoon
Flour, all purpose	3 ½ cups
Expresso, instant	¼ cup
Baking powder	1 ¼ teaspoons
Salt	½ teaspoon
Milk, whole	1 cup
Chips, dark chocolate	1 cup

Method of Prep:

Preheat oven to 325'f

1. Measure out all ingredients and place the dry ingredients into a 4 quart mixing bowl fitted with the collar attachment (if you have one, if not, you can pulse a few times to avoid the mixture from shooting out the sides of the bowl and onto your work surface).

2. Begin mixing on speed 1 just until evenly distributed, about 1-2 minutes.

3. Slowly stream in the melted butter and milk. Continue mixing until combined.

4. Add the eggs and continue to mix, stopping to scrape down the sides and bottom to incorporate any lumps or dry pockets. Mix for another 2 minutes.

5. Add the chips and mix on speed 2 for about 2 minutes.

6. Stop mixer and scoop into a prepared 9 inch bundt pan that has been sprayed with pan release.

7. Bake for 50 minutes before checking. You can check doneness by inserting a toothpick, wooden skewer or butter knife into the thickest part of the cake on a diagonal. If the item comes out dry the coffee cake is done. If not, continue baking in 5-7 minute intervals.

8. Once baked, let stand on the counter until cool to the touch then remove from the pan and dust with confectioner's sugar or drizzle with melted chocolate or Espresso Mocha Glaze.

~BONUS RECIPE~

Espresso Mocha Glaze

Sugar, confectioner's	2 cups	Espresso powder or Instant Coffee	2 tablespoons
Cocoa powder	2 tablespoons	Hot coffee, espresso or water	¼ cup

Measure and place all of the dry ingredients into a bowl. Slowly pour in the hot liquid of choice and whisk until combined and smooth. Pour, drizzle or stripe over dessert.

Baker's Tip: Allow the bundt cake to cool completely. Place a plate over the bundt pan and carefully flip the bundt and plate over together and set down on the counter. The bundt should drop out onto the plate all by itself - providing you were generous with your pan release spray technique. If not, you can help remove it by gently inserting a knife in between the bundt and the pan along the edges to help loosen it.

Granola

Yield: (3) Quarts

This recipe is very easy to make and it stores well for up to 6 months in the freezer. But don't worry, your granola will be eaten well before that point. It's nutritious and delicious and helps keep hunger at bay. Granola can be eaten plain as a snack or added to yogurt. You can even warm it up in a bowl of milk and enjoy it the same way you would a warm bowl of oatmeal.

Granola

Oats, quick	4 cups	Salt	½ teaspoon
Honey	1 cup	Cinnamon	1 teaspoon
Sugar, brown	1 cup	Nuts, untoasted	2 cups, chopped
Oil, vegetable	½ cup	Fruit, dried	2 cups, chopped

Baker's Tip – *Variations include but are not limited to: dried fruits such as apricots, blueberries, cherries, coconut flakes, cranberries, mango, pineapple and raisins. However, both nuts and fruits can be changed and exchanged to suit your individual taste buds and you can also add seeds such as sunflower seeds, pumpkin seeds.*

<u>Method of Prep:</u>

Preheat oven to 325'f

1. Scale out all ingredients and set the nuts and dried fruit aside together in one bowl.

2. Combine the remaining ingredients and mix together until evenly coated with both the honey and vegetable oil. You can mix bare handed, wear food service gloves, use a heavy duty rubber spatula or wooden spoon.

3. Spread mixture evenly and directly onto a sheet tray that has been generously sprayed with pan release. *Do NOT line with parchment paper unless you enjoy peeling burnt pieces of paper for hours from your granola…

4. Bake until golden in color checking and stirring every 15 minutes to evenly distribute the heat. Total baking time should not exceed more than 35-40 minutes.

5. Remove from the oven when finished and let cool for 10-15 minutes. Spoon the mixture from the baking pan back into the large mixing bowl and add in the nuts and dried fruit. Mix by hand to incorporate. Any large pieces can be broken up by hand.

6. Let cool completely, package and store until ready to enjoy.

Strawberries
& Cream Scones

Yield: (9-10) beautiful biscuit babies

Scones are individual biscuit-like cakes made from flour, fat and liquid, all of which can be interchanged with similar items to accommodate allergies and dietary requests. They can be sweetened, unsweetened or even savory. If left plain, they will indeed pass for an ordinary dinner biscuit but with extra oomph. Flavored with extracts, zests and additives such as fruit, nuts, seeds, chocolate chips or cheddar cheese, chive and bacon…. Talk about leveling up. I have several customers who place and pick up specialty flavored scones on a weekly basis. Most orders are for a six pack leaving three for my freezer which eventually find their way into my belly and then onto my hips and then I find myself joining the next Weight Watcher's Meeting., oink!..

Ingredients

Scones

Flour, all purpose	5 cups	Butter, unsalted	2 sticks, softened
Sugar, granulated	½ cup	Buttermilk	1 cup
Baking powder	2 ½ teaspoons	Cream, heavy	½ cup
Baking soda	1 ¼ teaspoons	Extract vanilla	1 tablespoon
Salt	½ teaspoon	Strawberries, fresh	2 cups, rough cut, chopped or diced

Baker's Tip: Buttermilk can easily be made by adding 1 tablespoon of either lemon juice or white vinegar to 1 cup of milk. Allow the acidic mixture to sit for 30 minutes allowing it to curdle before adding to your recipes.

Method of Prep:

Preheat oven to 325'

1. Scale out all ingredients. Either leave the butter out the night before so it›s at room temperature or warm it in the microwave until softened..

2. Place all of the dry ingredients into a large mixing bowl. Add the softened butter and mix together by rubbing your fingers until the butter is evenly distributed. Your mixture will be a little course.

3. Add the fresh fruit and loosely toss around in the dry mix to coat.

4. Now you can make a well in the center and pour in the liquids. Keep the carton of milk or cream open on the counter in case you need to add some more once you see how the dry absorbs the liquids. Depending on the humidity in your kitchen you may need to add a tablespoon of milk/cream at a time until your dough holds together. You don't want to be messing around with trying to unscrew the milk cap when your hands are covered in a delicious sticky scone mess. That's just wasteful and unnecessary.

5. At this point I mix the dough by sliding my hand down and along the inside of the bowl until it's under the center and then I lift it up and fold it back onto itself. I repeat this process until I have formed a type of semi round sticky ball in the center of the bowl. You're done mixing once all of the dry ingredients have been incorporated in. Don't forget to lift the ball and check underneath.

6. Turn the bowl over and allow the scone meatloaf to gently fall onto a lightly floured surface. Pat your hands into some of the flour on the dusted surface and start pressing the scone dough not meatloaf to shape it, usually into a type of rectangle/ovular shape and to the height of the cutter you're using.. The average size cutter is approximately 3-4 inches round and 1 inch tall. You can also get creative and use different shaped cutters such as a square or heart for Valentine's Day scones.

7. Dip the cutter in flour then stamp out as many scones as you can and place them one at a time onto a bare, unlined, sheet tray that has been generously sprayed with pan release. Any leftover dough can be pressed back into a rectangle and stamped until it's all used up.

8. Before placing in the oven, brush your scones with either egg wash, cream, milk, or juice. Any liquid will work. You're just looking to seal the tops, add to the caramelization and enhance the flavor.

9. Bake for 30-35 minutes and let sit on the sheet tray until cooled before removing.

Scones will hold nicely for up to 4 days at room temperature when wrapped air tight. They can also be sealed in sandwich baggies and frozen for up to 4 months. When thawing, simply pull out a package and leave it on your kitchen counter before bedtime or under your pillow like I do. They can be served at RT (that's kitchen code for room temperature) or warmed in the oven or microwave for a few seconds and then slathered with your favorite preserve, butter or refreshing lemon curd which is my personal favorite!

a party without
CAKE
is just a
meeting
julia child

Chocolate

This is the easiest chocolate cake recipe to prepare and it can be converted to suit any and all dietary preferences. The batter can also be used to make cupcakes, donuts, mini bundt cakes or my world famous funnybones.

Ingredients

Milk	2 cups
Vinegar, white	2 teaspoons
Sugar, granulated	1 ½ cups
Oil, vegetable	1 cup
Extract, vanilla	1 tablespoon
Coffee, instant	2 teaspoons
Flour, all purpose	2 cups
Cocoa powder	⅔ cup
Baking soda	1 ½ teaspoons
Baking powder	1 teaspoon
Salt	½ teaspoon

Baker's Tip: one of the easiest ways to change up the flavor of a cake or dessert is to exchange the vanilla extract for another flavor. For example, at Christmas time I substitute peppermint extract for the vanilla to make a candy cane cake. The instant coffee can be exchanged out for flavored powders, fruit zests or eliminated altogether without altering the final recipe.

Baker's Tip: ("pulsing" means to quickly turn the mixer on and off repeatedly like you would a light switch.)

Method of prep:

Preheat oven to 325'f

1. Measure out all ingredients and place directly into one mixing bowl.

2. Start by pulsing the mixer a few times to incorporate the ingredients just enough that they don't spill out over the top of the bowl and then adjust to speed 1 and allow the batter to mix for 2-3 minutes. This is the time you can preheat the oven and prepare your cake pans by spraying with pan release.

3. This batter is forgiving and can't be overmixed. In fact, the batter will become velvety smooth the longer you mix it which is even better because even chocolate cake doesn't like itself when it's full of lumps!

4. Bake for 30 minutes or until a toothpick comes out clean when inserted into the center of the cake.

5. Let cool for at least 2 hours before assembling and icing because a warm cake will always melt your icing and almost always fall apart when you try to move or stack it.

"I didn't start cooking until I was 32, before that I just ate cake" Julia Child

Lava

Molten Lava Cakes are always a show stopper. You can make them in any size cupcake or muffin pan that you choose, just be sure to adjust the size of the ganache ball that you pre-scoop and freeze to coordinate with the size pan you have chosen.

Baker's Tip – Lava cakes are easiest to remove when they have been baked in a pliable silicone mold that can be inverted and pulled away from the cake.. I use an extra large pink silicone muffin pan that I bought online.

Gentle Reminder:: You'll Need To Have The Ganache Balls Scooped Ahead Of Time Using A Black Handled Scoop And Frozen At Least 24 Hours Before Making This Recipe.

Ingredients

Butter, unsalted	1 stick	Eggs, large	4
Chips, semisweet	2 cups	Flour, all purpose	½ cup
Sugar, granulated	½ cup		

Method of Prep:

Preheat oven to 325'f

1. Scale out all ingredients and place the butter and chocolate chips into the bowl of your double boiler. Heat until melted, combined and smooth. Slowly whisk the mixture while melting and clean the sides to prevent the chocolate from drying out along the edges.

2. Prepare silicone baking muffin/cupcake pan by generously spraying with pan spray along both the sides and bottom. Dust lightly with cocoa powder.

3. Place both the sugar and the eggs into a mixing bowl fitted with the whip attachment and whip on high speed (somewhere between number 5-8 depending on your mixer) for about 3-5 minutes or until mixture is frothy and resembles that of soft whipped pale yellow cream or a sweet fluffy pale yellow meringue.

4. Lower to speed 1 and slowly fold the delicious melted butter/chocolate combo into the egg/sugar fluffiness and continue mixing on low speed until all are one.

5. Sprinkle in the flour and continue to mix on speed 1 until absorbed.

6. Divide the mixture evenly into 6 extra large muffin cups. I use a gray handled scoop for mine.

7. Press a previously frozen ganache ball, round side down, into each cake until it touches the bottom of the pan. The mix will rise up above the ball slightly. Be sure to smooth the batter over the ganache ball with the backside of a spoon so that it is completely covered before placing into the oven.

8. Bake for 30 minutes, no more, no less. The lava cakes will souffle' & rise up out of the pan just a little and appear shiny when done. Let them rest in the pan until they are cool enough to place into the freezer.

9. Once frozen solid, pop the lava cakes out by inverting and folding up the silicone baking pan.

10. While still frozen, place the lava cakes onto a coating screen and pour melted ganache over each cake allowing it to run down the sides to coat. I use the same size black handled scoop to coat the cakes as I did when scooping the ganache balls that I pre-froze for the centers.

11. Keep chilled or frozen until serving. Serve at room temperature or warm in the microwave for approximately 20-30 seconds which will allow the center to ooze out onto your plate once the cake is cut into.

Carrot

Yield: (3) 8 inch rounds = (1) assembled & iced cake or (12) cupcakes

Ingredients

Flour, all purpose	2 cups	Extract, vanilla	1 tablespoon
Baking soda	2 teaspoons	Carrots, shredded	4 cups
Baking powder	2 teaspoons	Milk, whole	1 cup
Spice, cinnamon	2 teaspoons	Sugar, granulated	1 ½ cups
Spice, nutmeg	½ teaspoons	Oil, vegetable	1 cup
Salt	½ teaspoon	Eggs, large	4
Raisins, any type	1 cup, unhydrated		

Method of prep:

Preheat oven to 325'

1. Scale out all of the ingredients above and place into a mixing bowl fitted with the paddle attachment and a bowl collar if you have one to avoid anything from shooting out of the bowl. If you don't have a bowl collar attachment, start mixing by pulsing a few times to avoid a mess.

2. Mix on speed 1 for approximately 2-3 minutes. Stop the mixer, scrape both the bowl and the paddle thoroughly and then return to mixing.

3. Once all of the dry has been absorbed into the wet you can turn up to speed 2 and let the batter mix for another 3-4 minutes. I actually don't even keep time on how long I mix my cake batters. I just mix until smooth.

4. Once the batter is ready you can spoon/scoop or pour into the prepared baking pans. How you get it in there is up to you.

5. Place in the oven and bake on 325'f for 25-35 minutes depending on which size pan and item you chose. Test doneness by placing a toothpick in the center of the cake on the bias or diagonal and checking to see that the pick is dry when removed from the cake. You can add time in 5-8 minute intervals as needed until done.

6. Allow the cake to cool completely before depanning, wrapping and storing. It's a good idea to cool your unmolded cakes in the fridge for at least 2 hours before filling and icing them.

Baker's Tip - Measure your carrots after you've shredded them to be more accurate.

Red Velvet

Red Velvet is similar to chocolate but NOT the same thing. It is equally delicious but a little denser and typically not as sweet. Traditionally, it's known to be iced with cream cheese icing but can be filled and iced with any flavor buttercream or icing oy your choice.

Ingredients

Flour, all purpose	3 cups
Sugar, granulated	2 cups
Baking soda	1 teaspoon
Salt	½ teaspoon
Cocoa, unsweetened	¼ cup
Oil, vegetable	1 cup
Milk, whole	1 cup
Eggs, large	3
Vinegar, white	1 tablespoon
Coloring, red	¼ cup

Method of prep:

Preheat oven to 325'f

1. Scale out all the ingredients and place into the mixing bowl fitted with the paddle attachment.

2. Attach the bowl collar to the mixer if you have one.

3. Pulse the mixer on and off one turn at a time for 3-4 rotations to prevent the dry ingredients from spilling over the bowl.

4. Turn the mixer on speed one and mix until all ingredients are incorporated, about 2-3 minutes.

5. Stop mixing and thoroughly scrape down the paddle and the bowl. Continue mixing on speed 2 for 2-3 minutes and then stop to check for lumps. If you have lumps, scrape down a second time and mix again until you don't. Continue with the 2-3 minute cycle until batter is lump free.

6. Once you're lump free go ahead and portion out your batter into the sprayed or paper lined baking/cupcake pans of your choice. Bake on 325'f until done or check at 30-35 minutes and add time as needed in 5 minute intervals.

7. Allow cakes to cool completely before removing from the pans. Refrigerate for at least 2 hours before filling and icing.

Vanilla Bean
Cheese Cake

Yield: (1) 8 inch Delicious Deep Dish Deli Style Cheesecake

A rich and creamy cheesecake. This recipe is a vanilla base that can be easily converted into any flavor cheesecake by simply changing out the vanilla extract with another flavor extract, zest, liquor or preserve and omitting the vanilla bean paste. The batter is super stable and can accommodate adding up to 1 cup of *drained* fresh fruit or 2 cups of dry ingredients such as chocolate chips, nuts or crushed candies. You can also swirl in fruit preserves, chocolate ganache or peanut butter. It is very easy to change up the presentation. Instead of making a round cheesecake try baking it in a square or rectangle pan that can be cut into bars or fill cupcake pans for cute individual servings. Once cooled you can get creative and top with icings, ganache, fresh fruit, cereal, crushed candies or just leave the top plain Jane.

This cheesecake can definitely stand on its own any day, all day.

It all works and it's all delicious!

Ingredients

Crust

Crumbs, graham	2 cups	Sugar, granulated	2 tablespoons
Butter, unsalted	4-6 tablespoons, melted	Spice, cinnamon	1 teaspoon (optional)

Baker's Tip: *Dried and processed leftover cake crumbs, cookies can be substituted for graham cracker crumbs.*

Cheesecake

Cream cheese	2 cups	Cream, sour	½ cup
Cream, heavy	1 cup	Eggs, large	4
Sugar, granulated	1 cup	Paste, vanilla	1 tablespoon

Baker's Tip *– Vanilla bean paste can be very expensive, extract can be substituted*

*Vanilla bean paste can be purchased in most health food stores or online for $10-20 per ounce. Or you can go old school and buy the beans, slice them lengthwise and scrape out the paste with a paring knife.

Method of Prep:

Preheat oven to 325'f

Crust

1. Scale out all ingredients and place the drys into a mixing bowl fitted with the paddle attachment. Let mix on speed 1 to distribute evenly.

2. Melt the butter until it's liquid and stream into the dry mixture while mixing on speed 1. Mix will resemble wet sand when finished.

3. Press into a prepared springform baking pan that has been sprayed with pan release and lined with parchment paper cut to fit both the pan bottom and sides. If you don't have a springform pan a traditional cake pan can be used but will need to be double lined with parchment to help with the unmolding process explained below.

4. Bake on 325'f for 10-15 minutes and allow to cool before filling the crust with the cheesecake batter.

Baker's Tip: *Cut The Correct Size Parchment Paper To Fit Your Pan By Tracing The Bottom Of The Pan Onto The Parchment With A Black Marker. Cut Out Along The Lines And Place Into The Baking Pan Marker Side Down To Avoid Transferring Marker Ink To The Crust.*

Cheesecake

Preheat oven to 300'f

1. Scale out all of the ingredients.

2. Soften the cream cheese by either leaving it out on the counter the night before or warming it up in your microwave for a few seconds at a time until soft.

3. Paddle the cream cheese and granulated sugar on speed 2 scraping as needed, which will be often. Add the paste/extract and continue until the mix is smooth and there aren't any lumps.

4. Add the eggs one at a time and continue to mix after each.

5. STOP & SCRAPE, STOP & SCRAPE. Make sure there aren't any lumps before going on to the next step.

6. Stream in the heavy cream and add the sour cream. Once both have been added, continue to mix on speed 1 for 2-4 minutes to combine.

7. Pour cheesecake batter into the prepared baking pan. Place cheesecake into a water bath and bake for 55 minutes before checking for doneness. Most likely you'll need to add more time. The time will vary depending on if you decided to make this a deep dish 8 inch round (approximately 4 ½ inches in height) or poured into a larger and more shallow pan. Test the doneness by shaking the pan lightly to see if the batter moves in the pan or sits firm in the center. Extra time can be added in 10 minute intervals if needed but not without checking the stability first. Don't be too concerned if the top starts to turn golden or a light brown. That can't always be avoided since you can't rush the time it takes to heat and fully cook the center. If you're bothered by the top being golden brown you can always cover the top with icing, ganache, streusel or fresh fruit.

8. Once the cheesecake is done baking, remove it from the oven but keep it in the water bath until the water in the bath has cooled completely. This helps to prevent the cheesecake from drying out and cracking on top. It also helps maintain the creamy texture and smooth mouth feel.

9. Wrap the cooled cheesecake in the baking pan and store in the refrigerator overnight before attempting to unmold. The key to a great cheesecake is in the chill. So just chill for at least 24 hours and up to 36 before attempting to unmold.

10. If you baked your cheesecake using a springform pan you can just unclip the side and remove the collar. If you used a cake pan you will need to unmold the cooled cheesecake by inserting a small offset spatula or butterknife in between the parchment paper and baking pan all the way to the bottom of the pan to loosen the sides of the cake and crust. You may have to make a second pass to help loosen the entire cheesecake. Place a cardboard circle or plate over the cheesecake and flip over and set on the counter allowing the cheesecake to release and drop itself down onto the plate then immediately flip over a second time onto a serving plate or cardboard which by doing so, now has the cheesecake on the plate right side up and ready for topping.

Baker's Tip - Sour Cream, Plain Greek Yogurt And Ricotta Cheese Can Be Used Interchangeably.

Vanilla

Yield: (3) 8 inch rounds/layers evenly divided

It isn't easy to make a bouncy vanilla cake without using shortening in the formula. I've devoted years developing this formula and have finally gotten the texture to remain soft enough to enjoy yet stable enough to support the fillings and icings used. It still isn't as bouncy as a dollar store box cake but then again, it doesn't contain chemical liquid shortening either. Making it both delicious and nutritious in that regard. This formula can also be used as a base for other products like bars, cupcakes, donuts, madeleines, mini bundt cakes, pound cakes and winkies (which are knock off twinkies).

Ingredients

Flour, all purpose	3 cups
Baking powder	2 teaspoons
Butter, melted	2 sticks
Salt	¼ teaspoon
Oil, vegetable	1 cup
Sugar, granulated	2 cups
Eggs, large	6
Milk, whole	1 cup
Extract, vanilla	2 tablespoons

Method of Prep:

Preheat Oven to 325'f

1. Scale out all ingredients needed and prepare baking pans with pan release, parchment or paper liners depending on the item you will be making.

2. Carefully melt the butter to liquid form and place into a mixing bowl with all of the other ingredients. Add the paddle and bowl collar attachment.

3. Pulse a couple of times to lightly combine the wet with the dry and then paddle on speed 1 for approximately 2 minutes.

4. Stop and scrape both paddle and bowl. Mix on speed 2 for another 2-4 minutes.

5. Stop and check batter to make sure that all of the dry has been incorporated and that there aren't any lumps. If there are lumps repeat step 5 otherwise proceed to the next step.

6. Turn off the mixer and scoop/spoon/pour the batter into the prepared baking pans/cups.

7. Place the baking pans into the oven and start the timer at 12 minutes for mini cupcakes, 20 minutes for average size cupcakes and 25-30 minutes for cakes. If needed, add time in 3-5 minutes intervals depending on the size of the item baking.

Barke's Tip – the cake will start to look golden in color around the edges and may pull away from the side of the pan as it finishes baking. To test if the item is finished baking you can insert a toothpick into the widest portion of the item. If the pick comes out clean the item is finished, if the pick comes out wet with batter add a few minutes and continue the testing process until done.

"Pulsing" the mixer means turning it off and on quickly multiple times in a row so that the mixer only turns about a ¼ rotation each time.

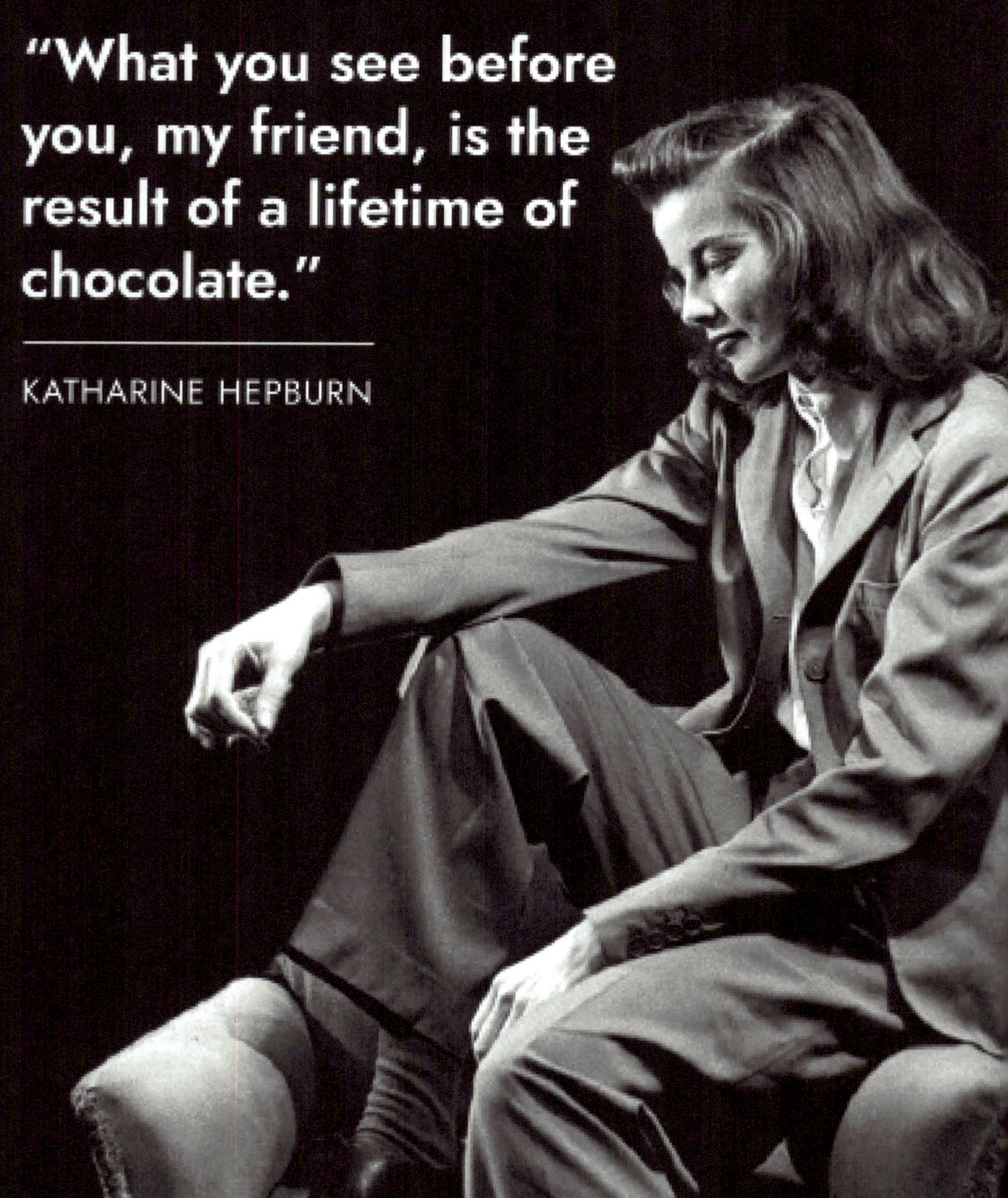

DESSERT BARS

"What you see before you, my friend, is the result of a lifetime of chocolate."

KATHARINE HEPBURN

Blackberry
Nectarine Oatmeal

These bars have a soft and chewy texture. You can interchange both the fresh fruit and preserves in these bars to create endless flavor combinations. You can also add dried fruit, flavored chips and nuts.

Ingredients

Butter, unsalted	2 sticks, melted	Salt	½ teaspoon
Sugar, brown	1 cup, packed	Spice, cinnamon	1 teaspoon
Flour, all purpose	2 ½ cups	Extract, vanilla	1 tablespoon
Oats, quick cook	2 cups	Preserves, blackberry	1 cup
Baking soda	½ teaspoon	Fruit, nectarines	1 cup, diced

Method of Prep:

Preheat Oven to 325'f

1. Scale out all of the ingredients needed.

2. Melt the butter until it is liquid.

3. Combine butter, brown sugar, baking soda, salt, cinnamon, and extract in a mixing bowl and mix on speed 1 to combine.

4. Add the flour to the mix and then the oats. Mix on low speed until fully combined with the above mixture.

5. Divide the flour mixture in half and press one half into a 9x9 square baking pan that has been prepared with pan spray and a piece of parchment paper placed inside to line the bottom. This little step will help to remove the bars from the pan easily once they have cooled.

6. Spread half of the fruit preserves in a thin layer covering the half of the mixture that has been pressed into the pan. Top with half of the fresh fruit.

7. Crumble the remaining dry mixture over the top of the fruit layer and press down lightly to help it sit in place.

8. Spread the remaining half of the preserves thinly over the top and again, repeat with fresh fruit. You're making a sort of dessert lasagna with this step.

9. Place the pan into the oven and bake for 50 minutes. Add time in 5 minute increments as needed (but no more than a total of 60 minutes).

10. Allow bars to cool completely before cutting.

Chunky Monkey

Yield: (1) 9 inch square pan, (9) evenly cut bars

SO EASY A CHUNKY MONKEY CAN MAKE 'EM

Ingredients

Graham cracker crumbs	1 ½ cups	Chips, semi-sweet	1 cup
Butter, unsalted	¼ cup, melted	Caramel nibs	½ cup
Coconut, shredded	3 cups	Chips, toffee	½ cup
Sweetened condensed milk	1 can	Nuts, walnuts	½ cup, chopped

Baker's Tip - *To make a chocolate crust add ½ cup of cocoa powder to the graham cracker crumbs and add 1 tablespoon of melted butter.*

Method of Prep:

Preheat oven to 325'f

Crust

1. Scale out all of the ingredients and place the crumbs into a large mixing bowl.

2. Melt the butter to liquid form and pour into the crumbs while mixing on speed 1 until well combined.

3. Press the mixture into the bottom of an 8 inch square pan that has been sprayed and lined with parchment paper. The crumbs will be sticky. You can pat your fingers lightly in flour to help prevent the stickiness or you can press in place with the flat back of a measuring cup.

4. Bake the crust on 325'f for 12-16 minutes and let cool completely.

Filling

1. Place the shredded coconut and chopped nuts into a large bowl and add the sweetened condensed milk. Fold the three together by using a sturdy rubber spatula and until well combined.

2. Add in the chocolate chips and caramel nibs, folding to combine.

3. Drop the chunky mixture into the chocolatey crust carefully by distributing all around in spoonfuls and press each spoonful down and into place and into the mound next to it. Continue pressing until the entire crust is covered and the chunky batter is even across the top. Careful not to lift up the spoon while pressing or you could end up lifting the base crust.

4. Smooth the top by flipping over the same spoon that you used to drop the batter in by gently pressing down while gliding the spoon back and forth across the top of the bars..

5. Bake on 325'f for about 45 minutes or until lightly golden in color.

6. Remove from the oven and let cool completely.

7. Wrap and store in the refrigerator overnight before cutting into squares.

Black Forest Cream
Cheese Brownies

Yield: (1) 9 inch square pan, cut into (9) squares

Extremely fudgy brownies topped with a cool and smooth flavorful cheesecake layer. Swirl in chocolate ganache, preserves or fresh fruit to enhance the flavor.

Brownie Base

Ingredients:

Butter, unsalted	1 stick	Flour, all purpose	1 cup
Chips, dark chocolate	1 cup	Cocoa powder	¼ cup
Sugar, granulated	1 cup	Baking powder	½ teaspoon
Eggs, large	3	Salt	¼ teaspoon

Method of Prep:

Preheat oven to 325'f

1. Scale out all of the ingredients.

2. Place the chocolate and butter into a bowl and heat over a double boiler while slowly stirring until combined and smooth.

3. Add the granulated sugar into the melted chocolate mixture and stir well to combine. This will also help the sugar granules to somewhat dissolve.

4. In the meantime, put the dry ingredients into a mixing bowl fitted with the paddle attachment and mix on low to distribute. Add in the eggs and mix until a thick paste like batter is formed.

5. Turn off the mixer and slowly fold in the warm melted chocolate mixture.

6. I strongly suggest attaching the bowl collar if you haven't already.

7. Turn the mixer on speed 1 and mix until all of the dry ingredients are well.

Increase to speed 2 and mix for 1- 2 minutes to smooth out any large lumps or dry ingredient pockets.

8. Pour the thick brownie batter into a prepared baking pan and let rest while you prepare the cheesecake batter.

Cheesecake

Ingredients:

Cheese, cream	2 cups, softened
Sugar, granulated	1 cup
Extract, vanilla	1 tablespoon
Eggs, large	4

Cheesecake Swirl

Ingredients:

Reserved cheesecake batter from above	½ cup
Chocolate ganache	½ cup (if adding)
Preserves, cherry	½ cup

Baker's Tip – *As If This Recipe Wasn't Fun Enough Already, Try Dividing The Cheesecake Batter Up Into Different Bowls Before Topping The Fudge Brownie Layer And Tint With A Little Food Coloring Like Pink Or Red For Valentine's Day, Orange Or Purple For Halloween And Red And Green For Christmas Or You Can Divy The Batter Up And Make Several Colors To Swirl In For A Tye Dye Design.*

<u>Method of Prep:</u>

Preheat oven to 325'f

1. Scale out all ingredients from the list above.

2. Soften the cream cheese by warming it in the microwave in 20 second intervals or by leaving it out on the counter the night before until it is at room temperature.

3. Place the cream cheese and sugar in the mixing bowl and paddle on speed 2 until there are no lumps. Stop & scrape as needed and continue to mix until the batter is completely smooth. *If you don't know what I mean by "cream" refer to the handy glossary that I have generously provided for you.

4. Add in the extract and eggs and continue to mix until well combined. Reserve ½ cup of prepared cheesecake batter for the swirl layer.

5. Pour the remaining cheesecake mixture over the double chocolate brownie batter already in the pan and lightly spread to cover with an offset spatula or back of a large spoon to smooth.

6. Prepare the swirl of choice by mixing the reserved cheesecake batter with the preserves and then drop by spoonfuls around the top of the cheesecake batter and use a skewer or butterknife to swirl around evenly. Or if you want a more prominent swirl, you can just drop spoonfuls of straight preserves onto the cheesecake layer and swirl them around the same way. However, preserves tend to be lumpy so I suggest "mashing" them in a bowl with a spoon first so you can swirl them easier once added to the cheesecake batter.

7. Place the pan in the oven and bake on 325'f for 55-60 minutes. Check the brownies by shaking the pan lightly and looking for ripples or movement within the batter. The brownies are finished when they remain solid in the center and without ripples.. They will also puff up a little higher than the pan when they are finished.

8. Remove from the oven and allow the brownies to cool completely before wrapping and placing in the refrigerator or freezer overnight to chill before cutting.

Baker's Tip – line both the bottom and sides of your baking pan with parchment paper before filling with batters. This step is crucial to removing the cut squares neatly from the pan before serving.

Double Fudge
Brownies

9 inch square pan

Yield: (9) evenly cut bars

These double fudge brownies are a staple in my little bakery. They are easy to make and bake into the most delicious fudgie bakery style brownies you've ever had!

It is also easy to incorporate substitutions at a 1-1 measurement and personalize your creation. For example, you can evenly exchange the extract and spice or leave them out completely. You can also use a rolling pin or food processor to crush and mix in candy, cereal, nuts, dried fruit or whatever suits your fancy. Your additions should be added once you have finished mixing the batter and just before you fold it into the pan. I often add 1 teaspoon of sea salt to the batter and then sprinkle some on top after icing. Try experimenting with different icing options as well like fudge, ganache, peanut butter, cream cheese, powdered sugar or preserves.

Another fun option is to change up the presentation. You don't have to only make pan brownies with this formula. You can also fill mini bundt pans or bake into thin layers that you can cut out with cookie cutters. I've even baked thin layers of this batter in round cake pans that I've used to stack in between cake layers before icing. Just remember to adjust your baking time so you don't burn the smaller/thinner cutouts.

Ingredients

Butter, unsalted	1 cup, softened	Eggs, large	4
Chips, semi-sweet	1 ½ cups	Spice, cinnamon	1 teaspoon
Coffee, brewed	¼ cup	Salt	½ teaspoon
Sugar, brown	1 cup	Extract, vanilla	1 tablespoon
Sugar, granulated	1 cup	Flour, all purpose	1 ½ cups

Method of prep:

Preheat oven to 325'f

1. Measure out all of the ingredients and set aside.

2. Place the butter, chocolate and coffee into a double boiler and heat until melted while slowly whisking until smoothly combined.

3. Add both sugars to the double boiler and continue to whisk slowly until melted and combined into the already smooth chocolate mixture.

4. Remove mix from the heat and transfer into a stand up mixer bowl with paddle attachment. Paddle on speed 1 while slowly adding in the remaining dry ingredients. (ps, if you don't like cinnamon you can leave it out).

5. Stop and scrape as needed, twice should do it. Paddle 1 minute after each scrape down. (this is where you would add in any special additions as mentioned above and mix to incorporate by hand rather than with the paddle so as not to crush your delicious creations).

6. Pour brownie batter into a 9 inch square baking pan that has been sprayed and the bottom lined with parchment paper.

7. Bake on 325'f for 35 minutes before checking doneness. If more time is needed, add in 5 minute intervals. Remember you can check the doneness by inserting a toothpick into the thickest part.

8. Brownies will feel firm to the touch, look shiny on top and begin to crack slightly when finished baking.

9. Allow baked brownies to cool to room temperature before icing & or cutting.

Cooled brownies can be dusted with powdered sugar or iced with fudge icing, ganache, buttercream, peanut butter, preserves, or any other flavor combination that you can come up with..

Baker's Tip - To cut brownies evenly, place in the refrigerator overnight so they firm up slightly. use a ruler to measure out the brownie size and press knife tip into the edge of the brownie where you want to cut. Turn the pan and repeat until all four sides have been scored. Place the ruler on top of the brownies as a guide and gently slide the tip of your knife from one side of the pan to the other creating a "cutting grid". Cut brownies following your grid.

– FEELING DOWNIE? EAT A BROWNIE

Peach Pie
Crumble

Ingredients

Crust

Flour, all purpose	3 ½ cups	Extract, vanilla	1 tablespoon
Sugar, granulated	1 cup	Butter, unsalted	2 sticks
Baking powder	1 teaspoon	Eggs, large	2
Salt	½ teaspoon		

Filling

Fruit, peaches	2 cups, diced	Cream, heavy	2 tablespoons

Glaze

Sugar, confectioners	1 cup	Cream, heavy	1 - 2 tablespoons

Method of Prep:

Preheat oven to 325'f

Crust

1. Scale out all of the ingredients.

2. Place all of the dry into a mixing bowl and mix on speed 1 to distribute.

3. Melt the butter and add to the mixing bowl along with the eggs. Mix until crumbly.

4. Divide the crumble in half and press half into a 9 inch square pan that has been sprayed and lined with a piece of parchment paper along the bottom. This step will enable you to remove the bars from the pan easier once they have set up.

5. Top the pressed crumble mixture fully with the peaches.

6. Cover the peaches with the remaining half of the crumble. Lightly press in place and drizzle with the whipping cream.

7. Place the pan in the oven and bake at 325'f for 55 minutes or until lightly golden along the edges.

8. Once baked, allow the pan to cool completely before drizzling the icing on top otherwise it will absorb in rather than sitting on top all purty like.

Caramel
Butter

9 inch square pan

Yield (9) evenly cut squares

An old fashioned favorite that's sweet and salty at the same time

Ingredients

Shortbread

Butter, unsalted	3 sticks, softened
Sugar, granulated	½ cup
Sugar, brown	½ cup
Sugar, confectioners	2 cups
Extract, vanilla	1 tablespoon
Flour, all purpose	3 ½ cups

Caramel layer

Caramel bits or chews	3 cups
Butter, unsalted	2 tablespoons
Cream, heavy	2 tablespoons
Sea salt	1 tablespoon

Method of Prep

Preheat oven to 325'f

1. Measure out all of the ingredients.

2. Place the butter and all three of the sugars into a mixing bowl fitted with the paddle attachment and cream until smooth, lump free and fluffy.

3. Add in the vanilla and flour and paddle until a loose dough forms.

4. Divide the dough in half and press one half into a 9 inch baking pan that has been prepared with pan release spray and lined with parchment paper.

5. Bake at 325'f for about 15 minutes or until lightly golden. Remove from the oven and dock with a fork to help deflate the puffed up dough and let cool. This step will also help the melted caramel cream seep into the bottom layer.

6. Melt the caramel nibs, cream and butter either over a double boiler or in the microwave, by heating 1 minute at a time and stirring until smooth.

7. Pour the warm melted caramel cream over the docked dough and sprinkle evenly with the sea salt.

8. Crumble the reserved soft dough over the caramel layer and press gently into place but don't flatten. Sprinkle with extra sea salt if desired.

9. Return the pan back to the oven and bake for 40-45 minutes or until the edges begin to lightly brown.

10. Let the bars cool completely before cutting.

Baker's Tip - If you decide to cool these bars in the fridge, you'll need to separate the edge of the bars from the side of the pan first with a butter knife or bench scraper to avoid the caramel from sticking to the side of the pan.

COOKIES

"You Won't Be Happy, Whatever You Do, Unless You're Comfortable With Your Own Conscience. Keep Your Head Up, Your Shoulders Back, Keep Your Self-Respect, Be Nice, Be Smart. And Remember That There Are Practically No "Overnight Successes"

Lucille Ball

Exercise is a dirty word... every time I hear it, I wash my mouth out with COOKIES

Brown Butter
Chocolate Chip

Yield: (26) Black Scooped Cookies

*"Dear Diamonds, We all know who
a girl's best friend is... Sincerely, Chocolate
Chip Cookies"*

Absolutely delicious and full of buttery goodness. For an extra burst of flavor, try adding a tablespoon of sea salt to the dough when you add the chips! These cookies also make great ice cream sandwiches.

Ingredients

Butter, unsalted	3 sticks, softened	Baking soda	1 ½ teaspoon
Sugar, brown	1 cup, packed	Salt	1 teaspoon
Sugar, granulated	1 cup	Flour, all purpose	3 cups
Eggs, large	3	Chips, chocolate, mini	3 cups or (1) 12 ounce bag
Extract, vanilla	1 tablespoon	Nuts, walnuts, chopped	1 cup

Method of Prep:

Preheat oven to 325'f

1. Scale out all of the ingredients.

2. Place the butter in a saucepan and heat on medium heat while keeping watch. This process can be very slow depending on your stove top and type of pan used. It can take 15-30 minutes to brown and caramelize completely.

3. Meanwhile, whip the eggs, extract and both sugars on speed 3 until they reach the ribbon stage which means light yellow, fluffy and thick.

4. Add the cooled browned butter to the whipped eggs and continue whipping until well combined, thick and frothy.

5. Switch out the whip for the paddle attachment and add in the remaining dry ingredients. Pulse a few times to incorporate then continue mixing until the batter is well combined and there aren't any pockets of dry ingredients left unmixed.

6. Pour in the mini chocolate chips and sea salt if you've adding. Paddle just enough to distribute them evenly throughout the cookie dough. Careful not to overmix or you will break down the chips and turn your dough dark brown. Still delicious yet not very eye appealing.

7. Scoop the cookies with a black handled scoop onto a sheet tray or into a storage tote. Chill at least an hour before baking or you can store them in your refrigerator for up to two weeks and bake as needed.

8. Prepare a sheet tray by lining with parchment paper and placing 8 black handled scooped cookies on the tray as shown below. You'll have to adjust the spacing if you changed up the scoop size allowing enough spacing for the cookies to spread.

9. Bake at 325'f for 14-16 minutes or until the edges are just starting to brown.

10. Remove from the oven and allow to cool completely before removing from the tray with a spatula.

Variations - Walnuts can be omitted or exchanged with another variety of chopped nuts. Vanilla extract can also be exchanged with another flavor extract of your choice. Both almond and orange extract work well to compliment chocolate chip cookies. You can also get creative and change up the flavor of this cookie by exchanging the semi-sweet chips for any flavor chip, ex: dark chocolate, white chocolate, milk chocolate, butterscotch, peanut butter, etc…

Baker's Tip – The browned butter can be prepared up to a week ahead of time and stored in the refrigerator until needed. Or you can omit this step completely and just use softened butter. The recipe will still work!

Whoopie Pies

Whoopie Pies are an old fashioned "comfort food" dessert that seem to have made a comeback over the past few years. I typically make these with a black handled scoop because it creates a single serve dessert that is both neat and uniform. However, they can also be scooped with a spoon. The filling combinations are endless. Buttercream and Cream Cheese icing work well and can both be tinted or flavored with extracts or zests. You can also line the insides with melted chocolate or preserves before filling.

Baker's Tip: For fudgy whoopies add an extra egg to the mixture.

Ingredients

Flour, all purpose	2 cups	Butter, unsalted	8 tablespoons, melted
Cocoa powder	½ cup	Eggs, large	1
Baking soda	1 teaspoon	Extract, vanilla	1 tablespoon
Salt	½ teaspoon	Milk, whole	1 cup
Sugar, brown	1 cup, packed	Coffee, instant	1 tablespoon

Method of Prep:

Preheat oven to 325'f

1. Measure out the ingredients and place all of the dry into a mixing bowl fitted with the paddle attachment. Pulse to combine.

2. Turn up to speed 1 and add the extract, egg and stream in the melted liquid butter.

3. Stop, scrape and then back to speed 1 it is while slowly streaming in the milk.

4. Turn up to speed 2 and let mix for 2-3 minutes.

5. Prepare baking sheets by lining with parchment paper and lightly spraying with pan spray.

6. Scoop the mixture with a black handled scoop and arrange on the sheet tray in 3 x 4 rows.

7. Bake for 13 - 15 minutes. Allow to cool completely before removing and filling.

Baker's Tip – If You Make 'Em Round They're Whoopie Pies.
If You Make Them Oblong They're Devil Dogs!

Life Happens, Chocolate helps

Cowboy Cookies

Yield:(30) cookies

Cowboy cookies were originally a granola type bar prepared in large batches because they had a long shelf life and thus, were given out to troops during the civil war to keep with their food rations providing them with extra calories and a quick burst of energy when needed.

Ingredients

Butter, unsalted	1 ½ sticks, softened
Sugar, granulated	¾ cup
Sugar, brown	¾ cup
Eggs, large	2
Extract, vanilla	2 teaspoons
Flour, all purpose	1 ¼ cups
Baking soda	1 teaspoon
Baking powder	1 ½ teaspoons
Salt	1 teaspoon
Oats, quick cook	1 ½ cups
Coconut flakes, sweetened	½ cup
Nuts, chopped	½ cup
Chips: Toffee	½ cup

***Variations** – any variety of nut can be used as long as they are chopped. Chocolate chips can also be exchanged with butterscotch, peanut butter, white chocolate, etc. Dried fruits can be added in place of one of the other additives..*

Method of Prep:

Preheat oven to 325'f

1. Scale out all of the ingredients.

2. Place the butter and both sugars in the mixing bowl and cream on speed 2 until light and fluffy. Stop & scrape.

3. Add the eggs and extract and mix to incorporate on speed 2. Stop & Scrape.

4. Place the flour, baking powder, baking soda and salt into the mixing bowl and pulse to combine. Once the flour has been mostly absorbed into the egg mixture turn the mixer up to speed 1 then 2 and allow to mix for 2 minutes.

5. Add in and mix the remaining ingredients one at a time stopping to scrape well after each.

6. Immediately scoop the cookie dough onto sheet trays or into a tote using a black handled scoop and wrap to chill for at least 2 hours.

7. Preheat the oven to 325'f and remove cookies from the refrigerator.

8. Place on a cookie sheet lined with parchment in a 3x4 pattern and bake for 18-22 minutes or until the edges turn a light golden color.

9. Remove the tray from the oven and let cool completely before removing with a spatula.

Flourless
Brownie

Ingredients

Sugar, confectioner's	3 cups	Eggs, large	3, whites only
Cocoa powder	1 cup	Extract, vanilla	1 teaspoon
Salt	¼ teaspoon	Chocolate chips, mini	½ cup

Method of prep:

Preheat oven to 325'

1. Scale out all ingredients listed above.

2. Place the confectioner's sugar, cocoa powder and salt into a mixing bowl. Pulse the mixer a few times to start then paddle on speed 1 just enough to incorporate the three dry ingredients.

3. Slowly add the extract and egg whites to the dry mix while still paddling on speed 1 until combined. You may or may not use all of the whites. The batter should be a little on the thick side when scooped. If it is a runny you will need to add in additional confectioner's sugar a tablespoon at a time and mix in to help thicken. Stop and scrape as needed.

4. Add in the mini chocolate chips and paddle for approximately 1 minute.

5. Turn off the mixer, remove and scrape the batter from the paddle to add back into the mix.

6. Scoop the cookie mix with a black handle scoop and place onto a parchment lined sheet tray that has been sprayed with pan release. Arrange in a 3x4 pattern.

7. Bake cookies at 325'f for 14-16 minutes.

8. Remove cookies from the oven and allow to cool for 30 minutes before removing from the parchment. If the cookies stick, they can be lifted from the paper with a spatula by holding the paper in place while sliding the spatula under the cookie to release the chocolate from the paper. Or pop the entire tray into the freezer for 10 minutes and then just peel the paper back while lifting the decadent cookie.

Variations – Any flavor extract can be substituted for the vanilla extract. Adding peppermint is very popular when making these cookies for gifts or platters at Christmas time.

"Without deviation from the norm, progress is not possible"
Frank Zappa

Ginger
Molasses

Yield: (26) black handled scoops

These are a soft and chewy blast from the past. I also use them to make sandwich cookies filled with lemon cream or sometimes process a few leftover cookies into crumbs and then press into the sides of an iced cake to coat or sprinkle on anything like plain greek yogurt and ice cream.

Ingredients

Butter, unsalted	1 ½ stick, softened	Flour, all purpose	3 cups
Sugar, brown	1 cup, packed	Cinnamon	1 teaspoon
Molasses	½ cup	Ginger	1 teaspoon
Eggs, large	2	Baking soda	1 teaspoon
Extract, vanilla	1 tablespoon	Sugar, sanding	Enough

Method of prep:

Preheat oven to 325'f

1. Scale out all of the ingredients.

2. Cream the room temperature butter with the brown sugar in a stand up mixer fitted with the paddle attachment on speed 1 until light and fluffy. Approx 3 minutes.

3. Stop, scrape and add the molasses, eggs, extract, baking soda and spices. Paddle on speed 1 until combined, scraping as needed.

4. Add the collar attachment to the mixer and while paddling on speed 1, slowly sprinkle in the flour and continue to mix until well combined.

5. Remove bowl from the mixer and scrape the sides down.

6. Scoop cookies onto a parchment lined cookie sheet and chill in the freezer for 2 hours or store in a tote and refrigerate for up to 3 weeks.

7. Before baking, remove cookies from the refrigerator and press the round side firmly into the sanding sugar to coat and then place onto a cookie sheet in rows of 3x4 providing you used a black handled scoop. If you opted to use a larger scoop you'll need to space out accordingly.

8. Bake for 14-20 minutes, again depending on the size of the cookie scooped. Remove and let cool to room temperature before lifting off of the cookie tray with a small offset spatula to serve.

Peanut Butter

Yield: (26-28) black handled scoop

Ingredients

Butter, unsalted	1 ½ sticks, softened	Extract, vanilla	1 tablespoon
Peanut butter, smooth	1 ½ cups	Flour, all purpose	1 ½ cup
Sugar, granulated	¾ cup	Baking soda	1 teaspoon
Sugar, brown	½ cup, packed	Salt	½ teaspoon
Eggs, large	2		

Method of Prep:

Preheat oven to 325'f

1. Scale out all ingredients.

2. Place the butter and both sugars in a mixing bowl fitted with the paddle attachment. Cream together on speed 1 until light and fluffy, about 3 minutes.

3. Add the peanut butter, extract and eggs. Continue to paddle until incorporated and smooth while remaining on speed 1 for about 1 minute.

4. Scrape down the sides of the bowl and attach the bowl collar. Add the baking soda, salt and flour. Continue to paddle on speed 1, scraping again if needed. Be careful not to overmix or the peanut butter will tighten up and make the dough difficult to scoop.

5. Scoop the cookies with a black handled scoop onto a parchment lined sheet tray and refrigerate for 2 hours before baking.

6. When ready to bake, place 8 cookies onto the sheet tray in a 3x4 pattern. Press each cookie with the back of a fork both horizontally and then vertically across to form a rough cross hatched pattern. You can sprinkle the cookies with a little extra granulated sugar if desired. Colored sugar works just as well.

7. Bake the cookies at 325'f for 20-22 minutes or until the edges begin to brown.

8. Allow the cookies to cool completely before removing from the sheet tray and serving or the cookies will break and you'll burn your little paws.

Variations:

Paddle in 1-2 cups of the following for 1 minute after the flour has been incorporated fully. Chocolate Chips, Raisins, Peanut Butter Chips, White Chocolate Chips, Chopped Nuts or even Carob chips if you plan on sharing with your best pup!

Peanut Blossoms - *Press an unfoiled hershey kiss into the center of each cookie immediately after removing the tray from the oven.*

Tip: *when making peanut blossoms count the number of cookies you scoop on to the baking tray and then count the hershey kisses to match. Remove the foil wrappers while the cookies are baking so you're ready to press into the center when you pull the baked cookies from the oven. If you pull the cookies out and THEN remove the foils the cookies will begin to cool and firm up preventing the chocolate kiss from pressing into the center.*

Peanut Butter Dog Bones

"If you love Pit Bulls raise your hands. If not, raise your standards"

These dough cut outs can be placed tightly on the baking tray. They might puff up a little but do not spread during baking so it is ok if they are touching on the sheet tray.

Ingredients

Flour, whole wheat	2 cups	Oil, canola	2 tablespoons
Baking powder	1 tablespoon	Peanut butter, smooth	1 cup
Milk, skim	1 cup		

Method of Prep:

Preheat oven to 325'f

1. Measure out all ingredients and place the flour and baking powder into the mixing bowl.

2. Paddle on low speed to blend.

3. Slowly stream in the milk and oil while continuing to paddle on low or speed 1.

4. Stop, scrape and add the peanut butter.

5. Paddle just enough to incorporate the peanut butter - DO NOT OVERMIX - or the dough will become tight and seize up making it difficult to roll without blowing out your wrists, inflaming your carpal tunnel and preventing you from walking your pup this week.

6. Wrap and refrigerate the dough for at least one hour.

7. Remove the chilled dough and place onto a rolling surface that has been lightly dusted with whole wheat flour.

8. Dust the rolling pin and roll out to about a ¼ inch thickness.

9. Cut with the chosen cutter by pressing the sharp side down into the dough until it is flush with the rolling surface.

10. Use a small offset spatula, bench scraper or butter knife to transfer the cut dough onto the baking sheet. Continue to roll and cut the dough out until all of it has been used up. You can add the scraps back into the dough and keep rolling and cutting. I even toss the small leftover pieces onto the baking tray and bake them without any complaints from my well groomed dog customers.

11. Bake on 325'f for 35-40 minutes. Let cool before feeding to your precious pups!

Do you know what dogs are? Have you met any dogs? No? Then allow me to introduce you to mine. These vicious and starved for attention Ye Irish rescue pups don't really care what shape the bones are in; they just want them and they want them now, within seconds of first sniff, and the less chewing the better!

Piggles Von Piglet

Jojo Chubby

Tristan William

Piggles Von Piglet

Piggles disclaimer: *Piggy likes to keep it real and enjoys changing up her ear style depending on her mood*

Now back to the recipe...

Once you've got this recipe down you can get creative and shake it up a bit. I cut mine out in different shapes around the holidays. You can also paddle in bananas, bacon, cheese or press in carob chips or chunky fruits. You can even ice them with more peanut butter, greek yogurt or carob butter.

The additions below can be added to the dough at ½ cup per batch

Mashed banana, Canned green beans, Plain greek yogurt, Pumpkin puree

Is your dog on a diet? Here are few low calorie healthy topping ideas that can be pressed into the dough before baking are:

Diced Raw Carrots – Uncooked Oatmeal – Cut Up Fresh Apples/Pears – Carob Chips

Extra bones – as if.... Can be wrapped and kept in the freezer for up to 6 months.

Shortbread

Yield: 1 & ½ pounds of dough (18 cookies)

This is one of the easiest doughs to make. It's also my favorite because it is so versatile. I use it to make my world famous painted shortbread cookies, cream pie crust, tart molds, cheesecake bottoms. You can also add ingredients such as mini chocolate chips, crushed candies, diced dried fruit or nuts before rolling out and cutting into cookies or using as a sweetened pie dough. This dough is also super easy to work with. I always keep a couple pounds in my fridge and throw it on the counter about an hour before I plan to roll it out so it's nice and pliable.

Ingredients

Butter, unsalted	2 sticks	Eggs, large	2
Sugar, granulated	½ cup	Flour, all purpose	2 cups

Flavor Variations – *Paddle in 2 tablespoons of one of the below to change it up deliciously!*

Fresh Rosemary Needles, Citrus Fruit Zest (grapefruit, lemon, lime or orange) mini flavored baking chips, extracts, diced dried fruits and or nuts.

Method of Prep:

Preheat oven to 325'

1. Scale out all of your ingredients and soften the butter by either leaving out on the counter the night before or in the microwave until soft but not liquid.

2. Toss the butter into your mixing bowl and paddle on speed 1 until smooth.

3. Add the sugar and continue paddling until light and fluffy, about 2 minutes.

4. While mixing slowly pour in the eggs.

5. Stop the mixer, scrape the sides and bottom of the bowl, clean off the paddle and then put the collar on.

6. Begin to paddle again on speed 1 and slowly add the flour via the bowl collar shoot until it's all in and a dough forms around the bowl leaving just the paddle in the middle.

7. Scrape all of the dough from the bowl and paddle, wrap in plastic and refrigerate until firm, usually a couple of hours or store in the fridge for up to one month before using.

8. Before rolling out on a lightly floured surface, remove the dough from the fridge and let it sit on the counter for about 30-45 minutes to remove the chill slightly and make the dough more pliable for rolling.

9. Roll the dough to about ¼ inch even thickness and stamp out your cookies.

10. Transfer stamped cookies from rolling surface to parchment lined sheet tray for baking. The cookies don't spread much so placement can be as close as ¼ inch to other cookies.

11. Bake at 325'f for 8-12 minutes or until the edges begin to turn golden. Baking time will vary due to the thickness of the cookie and how many times you open the oven door to check on them. Allow to cool completely before removing and decorating with royal icing.

Reminder: Your oven drops about 50 degrees in temperature each time you open the oven door.

Baker's Tip *"Be sure to use a bench scraper, flat metal or offset spatula when lifting your stamped cookie dough and placing it onto your baking sheet to avoid breaking your cookies"*

Fillings & Icings

You think just because you made a little money, you can get a new hairdo and some fancy clothes and turn yourself into a lady? Well, think again

Mildred Pierce

Chocolate
Ganache

Enough to fill an 8 inch cake, top a dozen cupcakes or warm as a chocolate fudge drizzle for ice cream. If you want enough to ice and fill a cake you will need to double this recipe.

Ingredients

Chips, chocolate, semi-sweet	3 cups	Cream, heavy or whipping	1 cup
Coffee, brewed	1/2 cup	Butter, unsalted	1 stick

*Coffee can be a regular brew, flavored, omitted or exchanged with another flavored liquid such as juice or liquor.

Method of Preparation

1. Measure out all ingredients and place them into a double boiler on the stove top.

2. Turn the heat on high until water comes to a boil. Lower to medium heat for about 10 minutes then turn off completely.

3. Slowly whisk the ingredients together, helping to melt the chips and emulsify the ganache.

4. Allow to cool completely before transferring to a storage container. Can be stored in the refrigerator for up to 1 month or freezer for up to 6 months.

Baker's tip: Ganache can be thawed by being left out of the counter overnight, in a double boiler or slowly in the microwave.

In order to fill/ice a cake the ganache will need to be at room temperature. This can be achieved by leaving a sealed container of ganache out on the kitchen counter overnight.

Bonus recipe

White Chocolate Ganache

Chips, white chocolate	2 cups
Cream, heavy whipping	1 cup
Butter, unsalted	1 stick

Method of Prep: Follow instructions from Ganache recipe above

*Try substituting peanut butter or butterscotch baking chips for the white chocolate chips in the bonus recipe for an extra special treat!

Pastry Cream

Yield (1 ½) Quarts

This is a smooth and rich creamy pastry cream that can be used to fill cakes, fresh fruit tarts, eclairs, Boston Cream pies (which are actually cakes) or flavored to make fillings for Pate Choux Swans and Profiteroles . You can even fold together equal parts of pastry cream with fresh whipped cream to create Diplomat Cream which is often used to fill oversized cream puffs. Any flavor extract can be used. I often change out the vanilla extract for almond extract or spiced rum when making Zeppoles' for St. Joseph's Day and Baileys Irish Cream to fill the ginormous cream puffs I serve at my annual St. Patrick's Family Dinner. This recipe is also the base for my world famous cream pies.

Ingredients

Sugar, granulated	1 ½ cups	Butter, unsalted	2 ounces
Corn starch	½ cup	Extract, vanilla	2 tablespoons
Milk, whole	1 ½ cups	Salt	1/4 teaspoon
Cream, whipping	1 ½ cups		
Yolks, large	10		

Method of Prep:

1. Scale out all ingredients and place into a large stock pot.

2. Turn the heat on low to medium and whisk both the cornstarch and granulated sugar together until dissolved.

3. Turn the heat up to medium/high and continue whisking slowly throughout the thickening process. Depending on the actual heat of your stove burner and your confidence level this recipe can take anywhere from 15-45 minutes to thicken.

Cornstarch is activated with heat and has to reach 203f before it begins to break down. Even still it needs to remain at this temperature for at least 5 minutes continuously in order to gelatinize and create stability within a product.

4. Once the pastry cream has thickened, remove it from the stove top and place it on the counter to cool.

5. Place a sheet of plastic wrap over the pastry cream and press it directly down onto the top of the cream by smoothing the wrap with your hand so that there aren't any air pockets. This will help prevent a hard crusty skin from forming over the top while it cools.

6. Once cooled you can remove the wrap and spoon the cream into a storage container and store in the refrigerator with a date matching that of the milk or cream that you used. Whichever expires first. DO NOT FREEZE. Unfortunately, pastry cream does not thaw well after being frozen and often tastes pasty and chalk like when you do.

BUT WAIT - THERE'S MORE!

Pastry Cream is also the base for any and all delicious and decadent cream pies!

Add from the list below or come up with your own tasty combination

Chocolate Cream - 1 cup semisweet morsels   Peanut butter - 1 cup creamy

Coconut - 1 cup sweetened coconut flakes   Preserves - 1 cup fruit preserves

Banana - 1 cup diced bananas

Get creative! Try lining the inside bottom and sides of the pie crust with fresh fruit slices, preserves, peanut butter or chocolate ganache before filling with pastry cream for an extra surprise that will wow everyone!

Lemon **Curd**

Yield: (1) pint

Cool and refreshing yet tangy all at the same time. Citrus curds make delicious fillings for cakes, cupcakes, donuts, pastries and fruit topped danish. They can be used similarly to that of preserves by generously slathering on top of breakfast scones or stirred into greek yogurt.

Ingredients

Juice, lemon	½ cup
Sugar, granulated	1 cup
Butter, unsalted	1 stick
Yolks, large	4
Eggs, large	2
Starch, corn	2 tablespoons
Zest, lemon	entire rind

Variations – Any citrus juice and zest can be used in place of the lemon to make your own flavor curd. Grapefruit, lime and blood orange all work excellent!

Method of Prep:

1. Scale out all ingredients and place them ALL into a small saucepan.

2. Begin by heating on medium while whisking slowly around the sides and then into the middle repeatedly to prevent the mixture from sticking to the bottom of the pan and burning.

3. It takes time for this mixture to thicken (anywhere from 10-30 minutes depending on the type of pan and burner you are using). The cornstarch needs slow steady heat in order to activate properly. Do NOT rush this step.

4. Once thickened, remove the pan from the heat and let it set until cool enough to transfer into a storage container with a lid. The mixture will continue to thicken as it cools in the refridgerator overnight. Label and place in the refrigerator and store for up to 7 days.

Baker's Tip - *Cornstarch needs heat (in the ballpark of 203°F) in order for "starch gelatinization"—that is, the scientific process in which starch granules swell and absorb water—to occur. In other words, if you don't heat your cornstarch to a high enough temperature, and hold it there for a long enough time, your mixture will never thicken.*

Peanut
Butter Icing

A favorite of the "golden child" in my family
especially when plopped on top of a Vanilla Cupcake

Yield: (1) Quart
Level: Quick and Easy!

Baker's Tip: *Almond Butter, Hazelnut Butter & Sunflower Butter
can each be substituted to make this recipe Peanut Free!*

Ingredients

Peanut butter, smooth	1 cup	Sugar, confectioner's	4 cups
Butter, unsalted	1 stick, softened	Cream, heavy/whipping	½ cup

Method of Prep:

1. Cream the peanut butter and softened butter together on speed 2 in a mixing bowl fitted with the paddle attachment.

2. Stop and scrape. Attach the bowl collar.

3. Turn on speed 1 and slowly add the confectioner's sugar.

4. Stop and scrape. Return to speed 1 and slowly stream in the whipping cream while mixing.

5. Turn up to speed 2 and let mix for 2-3 minutes.

6. The icing will be a little thick which is perfect for fillings and topping cupcakes. However, if you want it to be a little smoother for cake decorating just add a tablespoon at a time of whipping cream until you get the consistency you want.

7. Package and store in the refrigerator or icing can be frozen and thawed on the counter until soft. (May require whipping to smooth it out before using after thawing)

Meringue

This meringue is great for piping into small cookies or mushrooms and baking to garnish Yule Logs at Christmas. It can also be used to top a pie and either placed in the oven to browned by means of personal hand torch. This meringue can also be used to ice cakes which acts as a great alternative to traditional buttercream icings because not only is it light and fluffy but it is incredibly delicious! Any flavor extract can be used to suit your taste. Some people choose to use clear vanilla extract when making meringue since traditional vanilla extract is typically brown in color. Worry not, the whipping process will incorporate enough air that the brownish coloring will fade away leaving a white fluffy meringue. However, if you do want to color your meringue you can add a few drops of liquid food coloring while whipping until the desired color is achieved.

Ingredients

Egg, large	4 whites only	Extract, vanilla	1 tablespoon
Sugar, granulated	1 cup	Syrup, corn, clear	1 tablespoon, *optional

Method of Prep:

1. Combine all ingredients into a mixing bowl fitted with the collar attachment.

2. Begin mixing on a low speed and gradually increase to a high speed allowing the mixture to incorporate air and thicken...

3. Whip to until firm peaks have formed.

4. Meringue can either be spooned or piped on top of pies before baking in the oven to lightly brown the top.

5. Transfer to containers, cover, label and store in the fridge. Use as needed

Meringue will store up to (4) weeks in the refrigerator however, it will deflate and need to be whipped again before using in order to get back in shape.

Oven method - Place your meringue topped pie into a 350'f preheated oven and set the timer for 10-15 minutes depending on how toasty you like it.

The fun method - Set your meringue topped dessert onto a rotating turntable and light up your torch. Rotate the dessert slowly while you aim the torch flame at the meringue. You can control the roasting by how close or far you hold the torch flame from your dessert.

"Every Woman Should Own A Blowtorch" Julia Child

Fun Fact: *Vegan meringue can be made by equally substituting the egg whites with garbanzo bean liquid!*

Royal Icing

A simple yet extremely stable and versatile icing that can be used to ice cookies, decorate cakes and pipe flowers. You can alter the consistency by either adding more confectioner's sugar or less liquid depending on what you plan on using the icing for.. For the basic recipe below I use water but you can exchange it with extracts, juice, milk, cream or alcohol to enhance the flavor.

Baker's Tip: *Keep in mind if you plan to color your icing that the added food coloring will count as liquid and thin out the icing so you will need to add less of the measured water.*

Basic Piping Formula

Ingredients

Sugar, confectioner's	2 cups
Meringue powder	2 tablespoons
Water	¼ cup

Method of Prep:

1. Scale out all ingredients.

2. Place the confectioner's sugar and meringue powder into a bowl fitted with the whip attachment and mix on speed 1.

3. Stream in the water and mix until absorbed then turn up to speed 2 for 2-3 minutes to smooth.

Once prepared, spoon out the amount you need into another bowl that you will work out of and allow the remaining mixture in the bowl to continue mixing on low speed preventing it from drying out. This process does add some air to the mixture and it will slightly thicken the icing. However, you can thin it out as needed, such as when using it to dip cookies by just adding a few water droplets at a time until you reach the desired consistency. Or you can allow it to thicken up until it's stiff enough to pipe flowers and trimmings. Store in a sealed container in the fridge until needed. Sometimes the icing will separate but it's an easy fix by just whipping it up again in your mixer.

Basic
Buttercream

Yield: 1½ quarts

Enough to fill and ice (1) 8 inch cake or top (12 - 18) cupcakes

Not only is this buttercream formula quick and easy to make, it can also be made in varying degrees of stiffness depending on what you want to use it for. I use it for icings, fillings, flowers and piping. All I do is alter the consistency based on the end result I'm looking for. More on that after the recipe…

Ingredients

Butter, unsalted	4 sticks, softened	Extract, vanilla	1 tablespoon
Sugar, confectioner's	(1) 2 pound bag	Cream, heavy/whipping	¼ cup

Method of Prep:

1. Soften the butter and paddle on medium speed until smooth.

2. Attach the bowl collar, lower to speed 1 and slowly add in the confectioner's sugar while continuing to paddle..

3. While mixing, stream in the heavy whipping cream.

4. Turn up to speed 2 and continue to whip until smooth.

It's also easy to substitute non-dairy liquids instead of using the whipping cream. I often exchange the cream with almond milk, coconut milk and even fruit juice when I'm looking for a creative way to change it up and enhance the flavor.

The same thing goes for the fat portion. You can easily exchange the butter and replace it with a vegan variety. However, if you are substituting with margarine you will need to reduce the margarine amount to 2 sticks for every 4 sticks of butter because as it paddles margarine breaks down slightly and releases the liquid that has been previously hydrogenated during processing to make it semi-firm and able to shape into sticks.

If you add too much liquid the buttercream will break and you won't be able to use it as desired. But fear not! If you make this mistake just add in more confectioner's sugar until it stiffens up and voila! Just like that you're back in the buttercream business!

For example, if you're icing a cake you can add a little more of the whipping cream until you reach the consistency that you like. I prefer my icing to be light, fluffy and very smooth. You can also achieve this by melting about a ¼ cup of the whipped icing in the microwave and adding it back to the bowl while paddling. On the other hand, if you're piping flowers you'd probably want it on the stiffer side and would therefore add less whipping cream. You choose, you decide, you have the power!

Baker's Tip: This buttercream can be made ahead and stored in the refrigerator and should be labeled with the shelf life matching that of the dairy products you used for the liquid portion. It also freezes well and will remain fresh for up to 6 months in the freezer. It can be thawed out by placing it in the fridge 2 days prior to using it, on the counter at room temperature the morning you plan on using it or even for short bursts in the microwave. I set it for 20 second intervals and stir in between when microwaving. But that's just me, you do you!

Fudge
Icing

Yield: (1) quart

Can be used as a filling, icing or topping for any and all of your favorite desserts!

Ingredients

Butter, unsalted	1 stick, softened	Syrup, corn, light	4 tablespoons
Cocoa powder	1½ cups	Water, hot	⅓ cup
Salt	1 teaspoon	Sugar, confectioner's	4 cups
Extract, vanilla	1 tablespoon		

Method of Prep:

1. Scale out all of the ingredients.

2. Cream the softened butter on speed 2 until smooth and lump free.

3. Attach the bowl collar and add the cocoa powder, salt and extract. Pulse to incorporate and then cream on speed 1 until smooth and lump free.

4. Pour in the corn syrup. Mix on speed 1 to combine then stop and scrape the bowl.

5. Slowly add the confectioner's sugar and paddle to combine. Stop & scrape as needed.

6. Slowly stream the hot water into the bowl while paddling on speed 1. Once combined, turn up to speed 2 and let mix for 2-4 minutes. Stop and scrape as needed.

7. Refrigerate or freeze until needed. Thaw by sitting on the counter overnight. May need to paddle and fluff up before use.

Fresh Fruit
Preserves

Yield (1) pint

Simple and Sweet

Ingredients:

Fruit, fresh	4 cups, chopped	Juice, lemon	1 tablespoon
Sugar, granulated	1 cup	Cinnamon	1 tablespoon, if using

Method of prep:

1. Wash, pit and remove skin from larger, thicker skinned fruits like apples, peaches, oranges. Berries can be left whole.

2. Large fruits can be roughly cut into chunks. Smaller fruits and berries can be left whole. Fruits will break apart as they boil down. You can leave as is or mash them smaller with the back of a wooden spoon if desired.

3. Scale out all ingredients and place into a 2 quart sauce pan. Simmer on medium heat for about 30-40 minutes. Occasionally stir the mixture to prevent sticking while the lemon juice works to soften and break down the fruit allowing it to release its natural juice and pectin.

4. Remove the mixture from the burner, cover leaving a small gap in the lid allowing the hot air and condensation to escape. Once the mixture has cooled to room temperature, scrape off the top foam, if any and discard it. Remove cinnamon sticks, if used. Package air tight and store in the refrigerator for up to 3 months or freezer for up to 6 months.

Baker's Tip: To heat seal your preserves for dry storage be sure to follow your favorite canning recipe.

Simple
Syrup

Yield: approximately (1 ½) cups

Simple syrups are often used in bakeries to add or enhance flavor and sweetness. They also help maintain moisture in baked items. They are used in much the same way that infusions and injections are used in culinary cooking. Syrups can be produced quickly and in almost any flavor you can come up with. They store well in the refrigerator and can be warmed in the microwave right in the same squeeze bottle that they are stored in.

Baker's Tip – *When setting up a cake decorating or plated dessert station you can plan ahead and make and label several different flavor bottles and store in a cambro in the fridge that you pull out at the beginning of each shift to have on hand when producing popular menu items to order.*

Ingredients:

Sugar, granulated	½ cup
Water	½ cup
Honey, *optional	½ cup
Extract, *optional	2 tablespoons

Tip: *You can exchange the vanilla extract for any flavor extract, your favorite juice or liquor.*

Method of Prep:

1. Scale out all ingredients and place in a small saucepan.

2. Heat while stirring until the sugar granules have dissolved.

3. Add in the honey and or extract if using any.

4. Allow syrup to cool completely before transferring to a storage container or squeeze bottle.

5. Use masking tape and a marker to date the syrup. Store in the refrigerator, heat before use.

Baker's Tip – *To Apply To A Cake Before Icing – Poke Tiny Holes In The Cake With A Skewer, Fork Or Paring Knife. Warm The Syrup And Either Brush On Or Squeeze Directly From The Bottle. Give It A Minute To Absorb Into The Cake Layers Before Filling, Stacking And Icing.*

Baker's Tip: *Wanna Try Something Fun? Try Adding A Few Drops Of Food Coloring To Your Syrup Before Brushing Onto Your Cake For An Added Pop!*

Whipped Cream

Ingredients:

Cream, heavy, whipping	2 cups, chilled
Sugar, confectioner's	½ cup
Extract, vanilla	2 teaspoons

Method of prep:

1. Scale out the ingredients and place them all into a mixing bowl fitted with the collar attachment if you have one. If not, you're about to learn why you need one…

2. Start mixing on speed 1 until the mixture starts to slightly thicken.

3. Stop and taste your mixture. If you're happy, proceed. If you want to add a little more sugar or extract do so now.

4. Gradually increase to the highest speed you can handle without coating your entire kitchen in dairy products.

5. Whip until medium to stiff peaks are produced.

Baker's Tip – *Medium peaks are great for icing the outside of cake, stiff works well for filling cake and topping pies.*

"Whipped cream isn't whipped cream unless it is whipped by whips, just like a poached egg isn't a poached egg unless it is stolen from woods in the middle of night." – Willy Wonka.

Brown Sugar
Caramel Sauce

Yield: 1 pint

Ingredients:

Cream, heavy	1 cup	Butter, unsalted	½ stick
Syrup, corn, light	1/4 cup	Extract, vanilla	2 tablespoons
Sugar, brown	1 cup, dark		

Method of Prep:

1. Scale out all ingredients and place into a 2 quart saucepan.

2. Heat the ingredients on a medium temperature until the butter is melted and the sugar is fully dissolved.

3. Continue heating for about 5-10 minutes while stirring into a smooth consistency.

4. Turn off the heat. Add any additional flavor variations you might be using and stir to incorporate.

5. Allow to cool completely before transferring to a container. Sauce can be stored in the refrigerator for up to 2 months or in the freezer for up to 6 months. Thaw by leaving out on the counter or warming in a double boiler or microwave slowly.

Baker's Tip - *Vanilla Extract can be exchanged with any flavor extract.*

with any flavor extract and added when the caramel sauce is removed from the heat and set aside to cool.

~Flavor variations~

Coffee Caramel Sauce - add 1-2 tablespoons of instant coffee or espresso powder

Salted Caramel Sauce - add 1-2 tablespoons of coarse sea salt to the sauce or sprinkle on desserts

Chocolate Caramel Sauce - add 1-2 tablespoons of melted chocolate ganache or chocolate syrup

Boozy Caramel Sauce - add 2-4 tablespoons of liquor of choice

Cream Cheese Icing

Yield: (2) Quarts

An old fashioned southern favorite

Ingredients:

Cheese, cream	2 cups, room temperature	Sugar, confectioner's	(1) 2 pound package
Butter, unsalted	2 sticks, softened	Zest, your choice	1 tablespoon, *optional
Extract, vanilla	1 tablespoon		

Method of Prep:

1. Pre-soften both the butter and cream cheese by leaving each out on the counter the night before you plan on making this recipe.

2. Place the softened cream cheese into the mixing bowl fitted with the paddle attachment and paddle until there aren't any lumps. Stop and scrape both the bowl and paddle as needed to help remove any lumps. Continue mixing until smooth.

3. Add the softened butter to the cream cheese and continue mixing until smooth.

4. Add the extract and zest and mix just enough to incorporate.

5. Slowly add the confectioner's sugar and paddle on low speed until well combined.

6. Store in sealed containers and date to match the date on the package of cream cheese you used.

7. The icing can be stored in the fridge for up to 4 weeks and in the freezer for up to 6 months.

Baker's Tip – *a 2 pound package of store bought confectioner's sugar is approximately 7 cups measured*

EXTRAS

Why be ordinary when you can be Extraordinary!

Pie Dough

This is a great dough for everyday savory items like quiche and pot pies. You can even use it to wrap and bake roasts or tenderloins for your fancy dinner parties. It also works well for fruit pies and anything with a top crust. It is very easy to make and never fails. I always scale my dough out to one pound portions, wrap and freeze. To thaw them out just toss them in the fridge the night before you want to use them or onto the counter for a couple of hours before rolling out.

Baker's tip: I choose not to chill my butter or water before adding to the recipe. Instead, I mix all ingredients at room temperature then chill for 2-4 hours or even overnight before rolling out. The recipe will work either way.

Ingredients

Butter, unsalted	4 sticks	Salt	1 teaspoon
Flour, all purpose	4 cups	Water	1 cup
Sugar, granulated	2 tablespoons		

Method of Preparation:

1. Scale out all of the ingredients listed.
2. Soften the butter, yes, soften the butter and combine with all of the dry ingredients into a mixing bowl fitted with the paddle attachment and the bowl collar.
3. Mix on speed 1 just to distribute and slowly stream in the room temperature water.
4. Continue mixing on low until the water is absorbed.
5. Turn up to speed 2 or 3 for about 30 seconds and then turn the mixer off cause you're done.
6. Divide into two or three even portions and wrap. Dough can be stored in the refrigerator for up to 2 weeks or in the freezer and thawed as needed.

~ When life is too much, Just roll with it ~

1. Prepare your work surface by wiping it clean.

2. Lightly dust the rolling area with the same type of flour used to make the pie dough. For example, if you used a gluten free blend you will want to use the same blend to dust your work area and rolling pin to avoid the dough from sticking to your work surface.

3. It is helpful to have your pie tin or pie plate handy while rolling out your dough. Either can be used as a quick measuring guide when rolling out the dough circle ensuring its not too large or thin. You'll want your circle to be about 1 inch larger than the diameter of your pie tin so you have enough dough to cover the sides of the tin and not just the bottom.

4. I roll my dough out to between ⅛ - ¼ inch in thickness. To lift them off the counter you can either quickly fold in half and pick up and place directly into your tin or you can slide a cardboard cake circle under the dough and then position it over your tin and gently slide it into the tin while pulling the cardboard away.

5. Don't be concerned if the dough cracks or breaks a little bit. Luckily this dough is pliable enough that most times you can just pinch it back together with your fingers.

6. There are many ways to finish the edging. You can use a fork, the back of a spoon, a crimping tool or or not choose to crimp at all. The easiest and my favorite edging technique is to just press the thumb on my right hand against the dough on the inside of the pie tin toward and in between the thumb and pointer fingers of my left hand which are on the outside of the dough.

7. I coat the inside of my dough with egg when par-baking for cream pies. Feel free to skip this step if you want.

Quiche **Custard**

This custard will stabilize 2 cups of vegetables/meat and 1 cup of shredded/cubed cheese

Ingredients:

Eggs, large	4	Salt & pepper	½ teaspoon each, *optional
Cream, heavy	2 cups	Nutmeg, ground	½ teaspoon, *optional

Method of Prep:

Preheat oven to 325'f

1. Scale out all ingredients.

2. Place the eggs into a mixing bowl fitted with the whip attachment.

3. Add in the heavy cream and mix on speed 1 until the eggs are broken up and the mixture is well combined.

4. Choose and prepare fillings from the list below or create your own. This custard will hold a total of 2 cups of combined fillings from the protein and or vegetable listing along with 1 cup of cheese from the suggested list. Herbs can be added as dried, fresh or pastes to suit individual tastes.

5. Fill the prepared quiche shell with the chosen fillings and pour the custard over the fillings. Move the fillings around with a spoon to allow the custard to fill in the entire crust and surround and cover the fillings.

6. Bake at 325'f for 35 - 50 minutes or until firm when shaken and lightly browned on top.

7. Let cool before cutting and serving to avoid the slicing breaking when removing from the quiche pan.

(2 eggs per cup of liquid)(2 eggs per cup of liquid)(2 eggs per cup of liquid)

Quiche Flavor Idea Chart

Proteins
- Bacon
- Chicken
- Ham
- Ground Turkey
- Buffalo Chicken
- Salmon
- Shrimp
- Lobster
- Sausage

Vegetables
- Broccoli
- Mushroom
- Onion
- Peppers
- Potato
- Spinach
- Squash
- Tomato
- Zucchini

Herbs
- Basil
- Garlic
- Oregano
- Parsley
- Rosemary
- Fennel
- Chives
- Thyme
- Tarragon

Cheese
- Cheddar
- Mozzarella
- Provolone
- Swiss
- Colby
- Parmesan
- Romano
- Ricotta

Herbed Tart Dough

Yield: Approximately (3) 1 pound crust doughs

Ingredients:

Flour, all purpose	3 cups	Herbs, fresh	1 tablespoon, diced, *optional
Butter, unsalted	3 sticks, softened	Water, cool	½ cup
Salt	1 teaspoon		

If you don't have any fresh herbs on hand you can easily substitute 1 teaspoon of dried herbs for the 1 tablespoon of fresh or omit altogether.

This dough is stable enough that you can add up to ½ cup of grated or shredded cheese of your choice.

Method of Prep:

Preheat oven to 325'f

1. Scale out all ingredients and combine all of the dry into a mixing bowl fitted with the paddle attachment.

2. Paddle on speed 1 for a minute to incorporate the dry ingredients.

3. While continuing to mix on speed 1, add in the softened butter and cheese.

4. Stream in the cool water and mix until absorbed into the dough.

5. Remove from the mixer and portion into one pound rounds. Wrap in plastic and refrigerate to chill. Use within 5 days.

6. Roll out dough by first lightly dusting the rolling surface with flour. Roll the dough from the center out, turning often to help match the shape of the pan you are using. If cutting into individual sized shells, roll out into a large rectangle and stamp out with cutters. This dough is slightly elastic and will need to relax before cutting and shaping to avoid excessive shrinkage.

7. Once dough has been shaped into the baking pan of choice, dock the bottom with a fork, skewer or knife tip. Line dough with parchment and fill with baking beans or weights. Bake for 25-30 minutes or until lightly golden. Remove from the oven and allow to cool completely with the parchment and dough weights still in place.

8. Remove parchment liner and baking beans before filling. Carefully inspect the shell for any stray beans.

9. Empty baked tart doughs can be wrapped and frozen for up to 3 months. Thaw out by unwrapping and placing on the counter until the empty shell comes to room temperature.

Baker's Tip: Dried beans make excellent baking beans. They store easily in a sealed container and can be used several times before having to be replaced.

Glossary

Glossary

Additive - Miscellaneous ingredients added to recipes for flavor, texture and aesthetics.

Allergens - Any substance that causes an allergic reaction such as pollen, grasses, certain foods and medications.

Almond Butter - Almond butter is a food paste made from grinding almonds into a nut butter. Almond butter can be chunky or smooth. It may be raw or roasted and available in a stir or non-stir consistency. It makes a great alternative to peanut butter and people with peanut allergies. Almond butter also contains about half the saturated fat as peanut butter. Almonds are a tree nut.

Almond Milk - A plant based milk manufactured from the pressing of almonds that is creamy and light in texture and mildly nutty in flavor.

APF - aka: All Purpose Flour - Flour is made from the finely ground and sifted meal of any various edible grains. Giant steel or stone rollers are used to break and grind the grain. **All-purpose flour** is made from a blend of high-gluten hard wheat and low-gluten soft wheat. It's a fine-textured flour milled from the inner part of the wheat kernel and contains neither the gern nor the bran.

Baking Beans - Baking beans are used for blind baking pastry shells to prevent shrinking and blistering. Simply place parchment paper over your raw dough product and fill with baking beans. You don't need to buy expensive ceramic beads or marbles to use for blind baking. Dried beans work perfectly and can be stored after each use and can be used repeatedly without harming your food product.

Baking Powder - A powdered leavener containing a combination of baking soda, and acid (such as cream of tartar) and a moisture absorber (such as cornstarch). When mixed with liquid, baking powder releases carbon dioxide gas bubbles that cause a bread or cake to leaven or "rise". Double acting baking powder releases some of the gas when it gets wet and the rest when it is exposed to heat in the oven.

Baking Scoops - aka: Cookie Scoops, a handheld spring loaded kitchen tool used to scoop uniform sized dough and batter. Using a baking scoop helps to maintain product size, consistency and baking uniformity while promoting a shortened prep time and limits food waste.

Baking Soda - "Bicarbonate of Soda" is a powdered leavener used in baked goods. When combined with an acid such as buttermilk, yogurt or molasses, baking soda produces carbon dioxide gas bubbles, thereby causing a dough or batter to rise. Baking soda reacts immediately when added to water and should always be added with the dry ingredients before adding any liquid. Once the liquid is added the baking soda begins to work and the food product should be placed in the oven immediately.

Belgian Chocolate - Chocolate that is manufactured in Belgium, France. It is supposedly the richest, most decadent and smoothest of all chocolates. Some of the world's most famous chocolatiers and chocolate producing companies come from France with Godiva being number one.

Bench Scraper - aka: Dough Cutter, a flat, rectangular metal tool with a handle on top that is used to cleanly cut dough portions while measuring. Also used when cleaning kitchen work surfaces by scraping and removing dried food materials from tables and counters.

Biscuit - A biscuit is a flour based baked food product typically served with butter, jams and jellies.

Bowl Collar - aka: Spatter Shield, a molded plastic mixing bowl collar attachment that prevents ingredient spatter and mess.

Bowl Scraper - A pliable kitchen tool made of plastic or rubber used to scrape and remove ingredients and batter from mixing bowls.

Bread Pan - A bread pan is also referred to as a loaf pan and is rectangular in shape. Bread pans are used to help hold the shape of the bread load while the dough is proofing and baking. The two most common bread/loaf pan sizes are bread/loaf 8x4 and 9x5 inches.

Brown noser - aka "kiss ass" That one coworker that everyone at work hates because he always makes a it a point to let you know how favorable he is viewed by the boss and does whatever, whenever to keep in good standing with the boss even if it means spreading the cheeks in the back room.

Brown Sugar - Brown sugar is simply refined white sugar that has been combined with molasses. Brown sugar is available in light brown sugar, containing about 3.5% molasses and dark brown sugar which contains about 6.5% molasses.

Buckwheat -Originating in Mother Russia, often thought of as a cereal but actually a herb ground and used to make buckwheat flour.

Bundt Pan - A bundt pan is a cake pan that is shaped like a donut with distinctive fluted sides that leave the baked cake with decorative indentations along the sides.

Bundt cake pans are most commonly used when baking coffee cakes.

Buttercream - Also referred to as butter icing or frosting, is used for either filling, coating or decorating cakes. The main ingredients are butter and a type of sugar. Buttercream is commonly flavored with extracts or cocoa powder, however, zests, preserves and diced ingredients can also be used. It is also easily tinted or colored by adding liquid or paste food colorings. Buttercream can be piped, spread or shaped into decorative patterns by using decorator tips, spatulas, spoons or even paint brushes and skewers.

Buttermilk - A slightly sour tasting fermented dairy liquid left after butter has been churned and commonly used in baking.

Caffeine - An organic stimulant compound found in foods such as chocolate, coffee, cola, nuts and tea.

Cake Pan - A cake pan is a pan that is designed to hold liquid cake batter while it bakes into a cake in a traditional oven. Cake pans can be round, square, rectangular or oblong with heights ranging from 2-6 inches tall.

Carob - A tree grown in the Mediterranean region producing sweet pulp filled pods. The pulp is harvested, dried and then pulverized into a sweet tasting powder that is often substituted for cocoa powder in recipes. Carob is caffeine free powder that according to the ASPCA is not harmful to dogs since it does not contain theobromine or other harmful toxins found in chocolate.

Casein - A protein molecule found in mammal dairy products.

Coconut Flakes - Shredded coconut fruit, sweetened or unsweetened - the choice is yours, they work the same only affecting the sweetness of a product.

Confecitoner's Sugar - Powdered sugar or "XXX" as it was known in the early 1950's is simply granulated sugar that has been crushed into a fine powder with about 3% of cornstarch added to prevent clumping. Because it dissolves so readily, confectioner's sugar is often used to make smooth icings, drizzles, candies and confections.

Cooking Oil - Oils have been used for cooking since prehistoric times. In general, oils come from vegetable sources - plants, nuts, seeds, etc.

Cornstarch - Cornstarch is a common ingredient made from the starchy part of corn kernels. It only contains carbohydrates and not any proteins, therefore, it makes a wonderful gluten free thickening agent for desserts, sauces, gravies, soups and casseroles. Cornstarch needs to be heated to a temperature of 203' in order for the starch to gelatinize which is how it thickens a product.

Creaming Method - A technique used in baking to blend the ingredients with a softer form of a solid fat. Creaming also incorporates air into a product thus creating a natural rise. This process is most commonly used as the first step when making cookies. The softer fat, usually butter, is creamed with the sugar until light and fluffy before adding the eggs and remaining ingredients.

Cupcake Pan - Originally cupcakes were baked in individual pottery crocks. Many bakers still use ramekins, coffee mugs or decorative silicone baking pans. However, these types of pans are best utilized in small batch baking. Predominantly, and to be more industry productive, cupcakes are baked in muffin tins containing wells of 6, 12 or 24 per pan.

Dairy Free - Simply put, ingredients that do NOT contain any part of mammal milk. Mammal milk contains casein, lactose & whey. People can be sensitive or allergic to one, two or all three.

Decorator Comb - A cake decorator comb is made from plastic or metal and contains serrated edges or teeth that will "comb" the sides or top of an iced cake with parallel lines or into decorative patterned shapes.

Digital Kitchen Scale - A digital scale gives the most accurate unit of measure and is an important kitchen tool used in professional food service where consistency between production workers is imperative. Digital scales measure weight, mass, pounds, fluid ounces, grams and milliliters.

DMS - aka: "Dry Milk Solids" is powdered milk. Milk from which all of the moisture has been removed. It is less expensive and easier to store than fresh milk. It is available in three forms, Dry Whole Milk, Dry Nonfat Milk and Dry Buttermilk. All can be used for baking and are easily reconstituted by adding the desired amount of water per package directions.

Double Boiler - A double boiler is a large saucepan or stock pot that has been filled ¾ of the way with water and fitted with a large bowl on top. The ingredients are placed into the bowl for melting by heating the water in the stock pot. Commonly used when melting dipping chocolate or caramel for apples.

Dutch Processed Cocoa - Dutched cocoa is cocoa powder that has been treated with an alkalizing agent to modify its color and neutralize its pH leaving it with a milder taste than natural cocoa. It is most commonly used in ice cream, hot cocoa and baking formulas.

Eggs - All eggs contain different combinations of proteins. If a person can't consume chicken eggs they may be able to consume duck eggs. Keep in mind duck eggs are usually larger than chicken eggs. If you choose to substitute them for chicken eggs you may have to reduce the amount added based on the individual recipe and size of the actual egg.

Egg Replacement Powder - A form of an egg replacement that can be substituted in cooking & baking instead of using whole fresh eggs. A common ingredient for people who have an egg allergy or adhere to a vegetarian or vegan diet. Powders are reconstituted with water per the manufacturer›s directions.

Emulsification - (not to be confused with Mummification) The process by which two products are blended together to form one stable product that does not separate. An example would be milk and fat forming cream.

Espresso - A coffee brewing method of Italian origin in which a small amount of nearly boiling water is pressure forced through finely ground & packed coffee beans.

Espresso Powder - Intensely dark and finely ground concentrated instant coffee. It's not just espresso coffee beans ground fine. It's actually coffee crystals that dissolve quickly in hot liquid.

Extract - Concentrated flavorings derived from various foods or plants, usually through evaporation or distillation. Extracts deliver a powerful flavor punch to foods without adding excess volume or changing the consistency. Liquid extracts will keep indefinitely if stored in a cool, dark plac. Just ask the monster under your bed to store them in his favorite shoe box.

FIFO - Ingredient rotation system, "First In, First Out". This system helps to use up items before their expiration date and reduces costly unwanted waste. It can be used in a sentence such as: When working in my kitchen, if you don't "FIFO" you better "GTFO"!

Flour - Flour is a powder made by milling raw grains, roots, corn, beans, nuts or seeds. Flours are used to produce several products including breads, cookies, biscuits, rolls, cakes, donuts and cereals just to name a few.

Food Coloring - Dyes of various colors, most commonly blue, green red and yellow, used to tint frostings, fillings and doughs. Food coloring is available in both liquid and paste forms and in a wide variety of colors. You can also combine drops from more than one color to make additional colors and tints as desired.

Fruit - Fruits are edible seed-bearing structures that develop from the ovary of a flowering plant. Vegetables are all other edible plant parts such as leaves, roots, and stems. Fruit is a scientific term. Vegetable is a term rooted in cultural and culinary tradition. Fruits can be vegetables, but vegetables cannot be fruits. Ovary, did you catch that? We've all been eating fruit ovaries our entire lives,

Ganache - A rich chocolate icing/filling made of chocolate and cream. Both the chocolate and cream are heated until melted and whisked gently, combining until smooth. Butter is often added while heating and adds both stability and richness.

GFB - aka: "Gluten Free Flour Blend" A blend of several different gluten free flours resulting in a lighter and more versatile gluten free flour blend that can usually be interchanged with all purpose flours at a 1:1 ratio.

Gluten Free - Gluten is a protein most commonly found in wheat, barley and rye products. Gluten is the product that gives dough its elasticity. Not everyone can digest the gluten protein. If someone with a gluten intolerance eats a product made with gluten their body will identify the gluten protein as a dangerous substance and send out antibodies to destroy it causing severe stomach upset, aka: diarrhea, cha, cha, cha… aka: number 3, commonly known in my family as a "code brown", fa la la la la la…

Granulated Sugar - "White Gold" as it was known in the 4th century and Before Christ, once a luxury only the rich could afford, granulated or white sugar is highly refined cane or beet sugar. It is the most common form of sweetener for both table use and cooking. Granulated sugar is also available in cubes, tablets and a variety of textures such as superfine, sanding and castor.

Grunt worker - A person who is often tasked with all of the unwanted work that is considered heavy, repetitive, mindless and annoying also considered undesirable and beneath upper management's purview of what their elite work tasks should be. Respect the grunt workers. They are the ones who step up and clean up everyone else's bullshit and are almost always overlooked and severely underappreciated for their hard work and daily efforts to keep the workplace going no matter what.

Heavy Cream - A dairy product produced from the fat that has been skimmed off the top of milk during processing. Heavy cream contains a minimum of 36% emulsified milk fat. He ain't heavy, he's my brother.

Honey - A thick, sweet liquid made by bees from flower nectar, usually golden in color. Honey's flavor and color are derived from the source or choice of flower that the individual bees have collected the nectar from. There are literally hundreds of different honeys found throughout the world. The most popular/common honeys found are clover and orange blossom. Honey is a humectant which means it retains and preserves moisture. On a side note, the word "honey" has always given me a touch of PTSD because my second husband used to call me "bee shit"instead of "honey" because he insisted that the words meant the same thing and because he was an asshole.

Identifier - An established indicator identifying what the specifics of a food item are. An example is: By placing crushed peanuts on top of a muffin you are identifying that there are peanuts contained in the muffin batter and therefore alerting a consumer of a particular ingredient that might otherwise not be visible or known until after they have consumed it. Identifiers are important especially to people with food allergies.

Joe Frogger - A soft and chewy molasses cookie containing rum and spices, usually ginger, allspice, nutmeg and clove. Very popular in New England with the first recipes dating back to the mid 18th century. Not to be confused with that cute little frog in the 80's who was constantly trying to race across the street without being run over by an 18 wheeler. Not even sure if his name was Joe….quick, somebody look that up.

Kilroy - Kilroy was here is a meme that became popular during World War ll in the 1940's,created by American Troops who often left the doodled graffiti on walls to mark where they had been. He was also a big part of my childhood as my grandfather used to get a kick out of doodling him all over my sketchbooks.

Lactose Free - DOES NOT MEAN DAIRY FREE - it just means the product does not contain the carbohydrate/sugar molecule lactose but can still contain the proteins casein and/or whey and visa versa.

Margarine - A buttery spread made for flavoring, baking & cooking. Originally made from animal fats, today most margarine is made from vegetable oils. Margarine is often used as a butter substitute because it is readily available, cheaper than butter, and free from animal byproducts which is appealing to people with specific dietary concerns.

Meringue - A combination of stiffly beaten egg whites and granulated sugar. In order for the sugar to dissolve completely and produce an absolutely smooth meringue it must be beaten into the egg whites a tablespoon at a time. Meringue can be used as an icing or filling for cakes, pies and pastries or piped into shapes and baked alone as cookies, garnishes or discs.

Milk - An opaque colored liquid rich in fat, proteins and nutrients produced by the mammary glands of female mammals. Fat content is the only difference between the different types of cow's milk sold in the market. Whole milk generally contains 3.5% milk fat, 1% Milk has one percent milk fat, 2% Milk has 2% milk fat and Skim contains no milk fat.

Molasses - A juice produced from the refining of both sugar cane and sugar beets. The juice is squeezed and boiled to a syrupy mixture from which sugar crystals are extracted. The remaining brownish - black liquid is molasses. Light molasses is produced from the first boiling of the sugar syrup. It is the lighter and sweeter of the two. Dark molasses is produced from the second boiling of the remaining sugar syrup and is less sweet and much darker.

Natural Cocoa - Natural cocoa powder is extracted by a process where the cocoa fats have been removed from the chocolate nibs and the remaining dry cocoa beans are ground into cocoa powder and then packaged. Natural cocoa powder has a light-brown color and is naturally acidic making it a perfect pairing in recipes containing baking soda contributing to the rise in cakes.

Oven Mitts - Oven mitts are insulated fabric mittens or gloves that are used to protect your hands and arms while removing baked items from a hot oven or stove top. I'm lucky enough to have a BFF of over 39 years who is kind enough to hand sew me oven mitts whenever I need them. She's a real peach.

Pan Spray - Pan Spray is a quick alternate term used to describe Cooking Spray. Pan spray is a spray form of oil, emulsifiers and a food grade propellant. Pan spray is applied to pans to prevent foods from sticking during cooking and baking. Some sprays contain silicone which allow the cooked food to slip right out of the pan when inverted. Pan sprays are available in plain or flavored varieties such as butter or olive oil. Most are labeled as zero calories and all contain toxins..

Parchment Paper - aka: "Vegetable Parchment" is a cellulose based composite that has been processed to give it properties like non-stickiness, grease resistance, and resistance to humidity. It is commonly used in baking as a disposable non-stick baking surface. It should not be confused with wax paper which is paper that has been coated with wax. Parchment paper is used to line sheet trays and cake pans to prevent items from sticking and to and to keep the pans cleaner. Parchment can be used over and over again several times before it needs to be disposed making it very cost effective.

Paring Knife - A paring knife is a short bladed knife with a firm handle that is used to cut fruits and vegetables. The blades on a paring knife can be smooth or serrated.

Pastry - Various unleavened doughs which include a base of butter or fat, flour and water. An example would be puff pastry and croissants.

Pectin - A natural water-soluble substance found in various kinds of ripe fruits that is used for its thickening properties in the preparation of jams, jellies, preserves and pies. The gel-like pectin is added to fruits that don't naturally contain enough pectin of their own. Pectin only works as a thickener when it is properly mixed and heated with the correct balance of sugars and acids.

Preheat - Preheating is the time it takes for your oven to reach the desired baking temperature that you have set to bake a specific item at. All ovens will vary so there is not a set time to preheat. The average time that it takes an oven to reach the set temperature is between 5-7 minutes. You can time your oven if you want to know exactly how long yours takes. It doesn't matter much to me because I don't preheat. I simply turn on the oven, toss in my baking pan and add 5 minutes on the tail end.

Quiche Pan - A quiche is a French tart consisting of pastry crust filled with savory custard and pieces of meat, cheese, seafood and/or vegetables. Quiche can be served hot or cold.

Rolling Pin - A rolling pin is a cylindrical shaped dowel that is used to roll out dough evenly to different thicknesses. The two most common types of rolling pins are rollers, with handles and rods, without handles. Rolling pins can be made from wood, marble, metal and plastic and range in size from 6 inches - 18 inches in length with a dowel diameter ranging from 1 inch -64 inches. Rolling pins can also be hollow or weighted.

Rosemary - An evergreen woody perennial herb with fragrant rich needles native to the Mediterranean region. Used in baking as a flavor enhancer to breads, tarts and cakes.

Salt - "Sodium Chloride" aka: NaCl, A white crystalline substance that gives seawater its characteristic taste and is used for seasoning or to preserve food.

Sandwich Cookie vs Whoopie Pie - Sandwich cookies are snappy crunchy cream filled cookies and whoopie pies are soft, fluffy cake like cream filled pillow puffs of love - that's it, boom, drop mic, the end!

Sifting - Forget about it! I've never sifted in my life. Never have, never will. Although I might be known to "dust" the tops of pastries every now and again, you'll never see me sifting. Not gonna happen, not wasting my time, not talking about it anymore.

Spice -A seed, fruit, root, bark or other plant substance that has been finely ground and used for flavoring or coloring foods. Spices are distinguished from herbs which are the leaves, flowers or stems of plants used for flavoring or as a garnish.

Sprinkles vs Jimmies - Basically, where did you grow up? Because they're the same damn waxy donut/ice cream topping with a variety of names depending on where you grew up.

Starch Gelatinization - The scientific process in which starch molecules are heated causing them to swell, burst open and absorb liquids.

Sunflower Butter - A paste that is made from sunflower seeds and used as a one to one replacement for peanut butter for people who suffer from peanut allergies.

Sweetened Condensed Milk - A mixture of usually, 60% whole milk and 40% granulated sugar. The mixture is heated until about 60% of the water produced has evaporated. The resulting condensed mixture is extremely sweet and sticky. SCM is most commonly used in baked goods and desserts such as candies, puddings, pies, icings, fillings and cakes.

Tempering - A term used in baking that describes how to effectively combine two or more ingredients being held at different starting temperatures in order to create a stabilized product with one solid temperature upon completion of the process.

Traditional Foods - Generally food products that contain meats, dairy, wheat, rye, barley, oils, fats, butters, etc… generally foods that a person without food allergy concerns would consume and enjoy.

Tree Nut - Nuts that are grown on trees. This mostly comes up regarding allergies. A tree nut allergy is a hypersensitivity to dietary substances found in nuts and edible seeds causing an overreaction to the body's immune system that may lead to severe physical symptoms. Many people are allergic to peanuts, which are not a tree nut but rather a legume. The most common tree nuts are: almonds, brazil nuts, cashews, chestnuts, filberts/hazelnuts, macadamia nuts, pecans, pistachios, shea nuts and walnuts.

Variable Measure - A variable measure occurs when specific food groups consisting of multiple options within the group weighing different amounts are converted between the units of measure and can't be guaranteed a set weight. For example: a cup of mashed bananas and a cup of diced strawberries have different weights when converting to ounces and grams.

Vegan - A person that does not consume any food products derived from animals and who typically does not use any other animal products.

Vegan Diet - A vegan diet is a firmly vegetarian diet. Besides not eating meat, a vegan does not consume any other product that is derived from an animal source, including but not limited to, eggs, honey, gelatin or dairy products.

Whipping Cream - A dairy product produced from the fat that is skimmed off the top of milk during processing. Whipping cream contains 30-36% of emulsified milk fat.

Whey - A protein molecule found in mammal dairy products. It is the remaining liquid after milk has been strained or curdled.

Whisk - A whisk is a kitchen utensil that is used to blend ingredients smoothly or to incorporate air into a mixture which is a process known as whipping. Whisks are usually made from metal and contain a firm handle and several hooped tines. Whisks can be as small as 3 inches in length and as long as 18 inches in length.

Xanthan Gum - A food additive that has been created from fermentation which is used as a thickening agent helping to prevent foods from separating. It is commonly used in gluten free bread production as a stabilizer for the elastic bands that would normally be created with the presence of gluten.

Yeast, Baker's - Baker's yeast is the common name for the strains of fresh packed wet cake yeast commonly used in baking bread and other bakery products. Yeast serves as a leavening agent which causes the bread to rise, expand and become lighter and softer.

Zester - A zester is a metal kitchen tool usually rectangular in shape consisting of sharpened perforated fluted metal holes with a solid handle. Zesters are used to scrape the rind off a piece of fruit and deposit it onto a piece of wax paper in tiny dried pieces that will be used to enhance a food product's color and flavor.

Common **Bakery** Tools

Paddle

Wire Whip

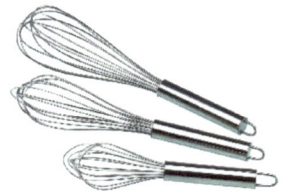
Whisks

Dough Hook

Stand Up Mixer, 4.5 quart

Bench Scraper

Offset Spatula

Decorator Comb

Mixing Bowls

Sheet Pan

Baking Scoops

Liquid Measure

Dry Measuring Cups

Measuring Spoons

Zester

Cake Turntable

Rolling Pin   **Rubber Spatulas**   **Oven Mitts**   **Bundt Pan**

Double Boiler   **Cupcake Pan**   **Cake Baking Pans**   **Digital Kitchen Scale**

Bread Pan   **Quiche Pan**   **Paring Knife**   **Cutting Board**

Bowl Collar

Cake Cutting Guide

Celebration cake cutting guide (2" x 2" pieces):

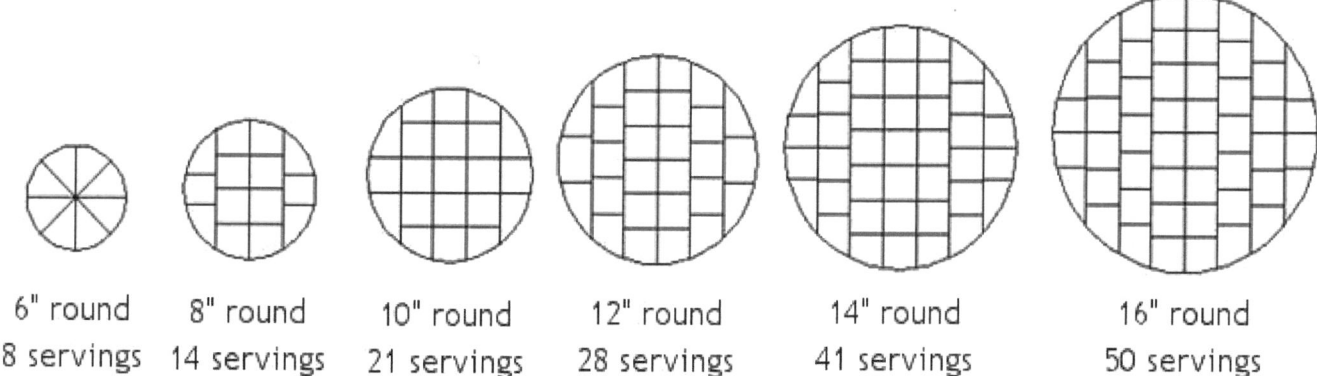

6" round	8" round	10" round	12" round	14" round	16" round
8 servings	14 servings	21 servings	28 servings	41 servings	50 servings

Wedding cake cutting guide (1" x 2" pieces):

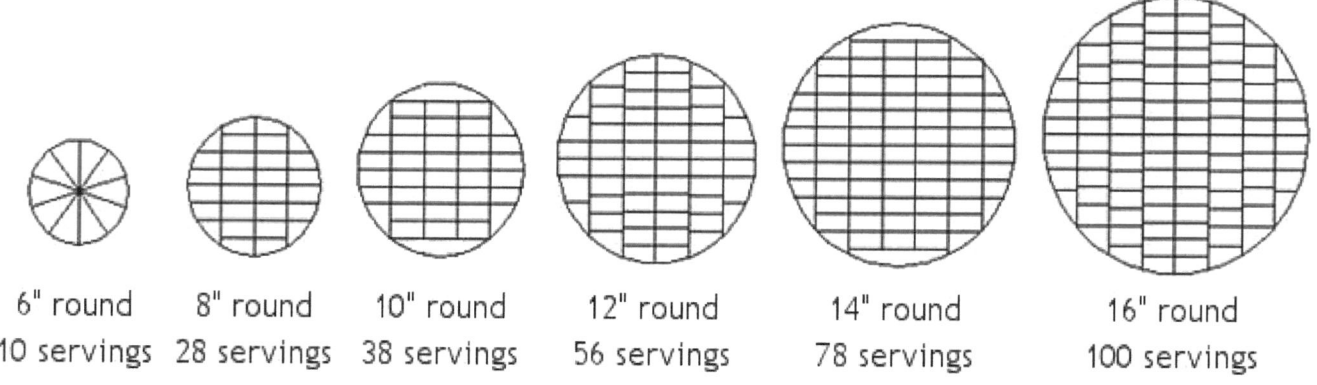

6" round	8" round	10" round	12" round	14" round	16" round
10 servings	28 servings	38 servings	56 servings	78 servings	100 servings

Thank you for buying this book!